NAKED GHOSTS

NAKED GHOSTS

INTIMATE STORIES FROM THE FILES OF A SEX THERAPIST

Carol G. Wells

PRENTICE
HALL
PRESS

New York   London   Toronto   Sydney
Tokyo   Singapore

Money, John and Anke Ehrhardt, *Man & Woman Boy & Girl*, The John Hopkins University Press, Baltimore/London, 1978, p. 20.

This book is the work product of Carol Wells' experience through the years as a therapist. Each of these case histories is a composite of people she has known and worked with throughout her career. Names of the patients described in the case histories have been changed.

PRENTICE HALL PRESS
15 Columbus Circle
New York, NY 10023

PRENTICE HALL PRESS and colophons are registered trademarks of Simon & Schuster, Inc.

Library of Congress Cataloging-in-Publication Data

Wells, Carol G., 1944–
  Naked ghosts : intimate stories from the files of a sex therapist
/ Carol G. Wells.
    p. cm.
  ISBN 0-13-612169-1
  1. Sex therapy—Case studies.   2. Psychosexual disorders—Case
studies. I. Title.
RC557.W45 1991
616.85'830651—dc20   90-48297
                                                            CIP

Designed by Richard Oriolo

Manufactured in the United States of America

10 9 8 7 6 5 4 3 2 1

First Edition

*To my patients,
all of whom have taught
me about the importance of
safeguarding in childhood the
precious gift of sexuality. And to future
generations of children for whom
I hope this gift will
be protected.*

Acknowledgments

To Jon K. Meyer, M.D., who did his best to teach me the skills of being a good therapist and to John Money, Ph.D., whose writings have greatly influenced my thinking.

Contents

INTRODUCTION   *xi*

GREG   *1*

HILARY   *40*

MITCH   *91*

JACQUELINE   *140*

DARLENE   *184*

Introduction

I had the idea for this book more than eight years ago. I had been a sex therapist for only a short period of time but was already acutely aware of our lack of understanding about how human sexuality evolves. As I listened to my patients' stories, I knew they had something important to say to all of us on this subject, and I wanted to be the one to put their message out to the world. As most things do in life, it took me longer than I intended. The message, however, is still relevant, as we have progressed very little in the last decade in our understanding of human sexual development.

There is nothing that makes adults more uncomfortable than the notion that children have sexual thoughts, feelings, and bodily reactions. Adults' discomfort is passed on to their children. As Marty Klein so astutely said in his book *Sexual Secrets*, whether you like it or not, you educate your children about sex every day. "Just as your children observe your table manners every time you eat with them, they also observe your message about sexuality . . . sex education isn't an event, it's a continuous process.''

Most parents, because they understand so little about sexual development, think they're doing an acceptable job teaching their children about sex. They confuse sexual development with sex education and think all that children eventually need to know is how babies are made. But sexual development consists of much more than reproductive biology.

Preparation for healthy adult sexual functioning begins at the moment of conception. Prenatal hormones are setting the stage, preparing the foundation. Once we are born, everything we experience contributes to a positive or a negative feeling about who we will be as fully functioning sexual adults. Infant boys have erections, infant girls vaginal lubrication. Infants, toddlers, children, and preadolescents, male and female, experience arousal and even orgasms from both erotic visual stimulation and physical touch. All of this is perfectly natural and is nature's way of preparing for later sexual functioning.

When I speak to parent groups about sexual development, I ask them to make a ''wish list'' for their children of the attitudes and behaviors they would like them to have as adults. The list varies little. Each time, parents include such qualities as consideration, respect, commitment, knowledge about what arouses and pleases the opposite sex, lack of inhibition, patience, freedom from guilt and shame, and last, but certainly not least, the ability to communicate openly and honestly about sex. What always stumps these parents is my next question: What specifically have you done to ensure that your child grows up with these qualities?

In a society that is uncomfortable with sex, if parents do nothing to counteract the societal message, children will tend to grow up as ignorant, silent, sexist, inhibited, guilty, and shameful. And if parents compound the societal message with their own negative feelings about sexuality, children will grow up sexually dysfunctional or even sexually destructive. The stories in this book illustrate how this happens.

Since life has done it for me, I have not needed to invent these plots. The childhood experiences and family reactions in all of these stories have remained consistent with reality. I have, however, considerably changed the family, personal, and background descriptions to protect the privacy of my patients. In all cases, composites of several patients were used.

Sex therapy is mainly talk therapy. A lot of the talking focuses on sexual development. It's not unusual for people to block out painful and unhappy memories. Because guilt and shame surround sexual memories, many people require considerable time and support to recall these memories. For the most part, recalling them is necessary to letting them go—a prerequisite for healing.

It's virtually impossible to be an adult in America and not have sexual secrets—naked ghosts that continue to haunt you and keep you from experiencing your full sexual potential. The future, however, holds the possibility of eradicating most of these ghosts for our children. It is my hope that the stories in this book will dramatically serve to point out how necessary it is that we come to understand and accept sexual thoughts, feelings, and bodily reactions in childhood.

NAKED GHOSTS

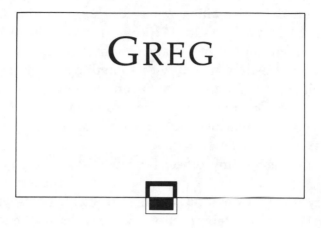

GREG

THE PRICE OF A SECOND CHANCE

While standing at the mailboxes in the lobby of my office building, I routinely go through all my mail quickly before opening any of it, dropping what I know to be junk mail in a large nearby trash can obviously intended for that purpose. On this particular day, I immediately noticed a large manila envelope. It was heavy, as if containing a workbook, so I turned it over to look at the return address, expecting to see the name of an organization from which I had ordered something. But there wasn't any return name or address, only the words *Private and Confidential* written in a bold, black scribble across the front.

I looked at my watch and felt a slight pang of conflict. I was a little behind schedule and didn't have time to satisfy my curiosity about what was inside. I slipped the envelope in my briefcase with the rest of the mail. Then, as if some other person had taken over my mind and made a different decision, I found myself taking it out again. It was only as

I turned it over to open it that I noticed it had been securely taped closed with mailing tape—the cantankerous brown kind that has filaments in it. I knew I was in for a battle, my frustration mounting because I simply didn't have time to get in a wrestling match with something as unrelenting as mailing tape. Deciding to surrender without a fight, I returned the envelope to my case and headed for my office where I knew a pair of scissors would easily make me victorious.

When I reached my office, however, my first patient of the afternoon was already waiting, and of necessity I had to delay the confrontation and my curiosity. I was soon to discover, unfortunately, that out of sight did not mean out of mind. Brief thoughts about the mysterious envelope occasionally crept into my mind during the session, and I was glad when I finally had the scissors in my hand and the envelope opened.

At first I thought it was a typed manuscript of someone's book. But the cover letter, also typed but unsigned, told me I was wrong. The letter read:

> I'm scheduled to see you next week for the first time. I've never talked to anyone about this and didn't know if I would be able to tell you either. So, I'm sending my thoughts on ahead of me. I realize they are scattered and probably appear more like the ramblings of a crazy person. Once I entertained the idea of seeking help, I took to writing down my thoughts as they came to me. I hope by reading this you will understand how difficult it was for me to make the call to your office. I'm also hoping my courage will stay with me until we meet in person.

On a few occasions I've had patients send letters to me in advance of their appointments, telling me a little about themselves and outlining what they think their problems are. But I'd never received anything like this. The loose, typed pages weren't numbered but I estimated the total to be around twenty-five. I scanned the front page and immediately knew that I would be in for some interesting reading and that my patient would prove to be a challenging one. As I slipped the pages back into the envelope and placed it back in my briefcase, the earlier feeling of urgency to know what was inside was replaced with anticipation, in much the same way that you look forward to returning to a really absorbing book.

Later that evening I was able to turn my full attention to the pages my new patient had mailed me. As I read, I felt as if I were being let into a very private world, a world premised upon secrecy. In fact, the more I read, the more I understood it was a world whose very existence depended upon secrecy.

Tuesday, January 9

I was in my car and headed toward my next client, my thoughts directed toward rehearsing the sales pitch I'm to make on our new list of wines. Suddenly, the goddamn image is inside my head. Where does it come from? Get the hell out, I told it. But it doesn't listen to me. It never does. Before I knew it, I was on the street where I know there is an adult bookstore. I told myself I'm going to drive by, that I won't stop. The words are useless because I stop anyway. Shit, I know if I stop I might screw up the sale. The client I'm expected to meet hates getting behind his tightly controlled schedule. But logic is useless with me when I'm out of control. When the images come, I'm always out of control.

Each time this happens, I promise myself it will be the last. What a waste of time. How can I be so stupid to keep taking chances on ruining my career? What's even more stupid is that I'm risking my life again and again. I get so angry sometimes that I think I'd like to dynamite the images out of my head. It pisses me off that I can't be like other people who can control their behavior through rational thought.

What's the matter with me anyway? Was I born this way? Am I doomed to be driven forever by these images? I feel possessed by my thoughts, devils dancing inside my head. It's only after I get off that they go away for awhile. But they always come back to torment me.

This morning I read a column in the newspaper written by a sex therapist. It was about a sex addict who had a compulsive need to peep into windows, hoping to find a woman in the process of undressing. Except for the compulsive part, this problem doesn't sound like mine. Yet, I wonder whether a sex therapist could help me. For fifteen years I've been shut up tight about this. I just don't see myself ever being able to admit this to anyone.

I feel foolish writing this diary. Reading the column this morning, it seemed like a good idea. But I've never been much of a writer and it seems so juvenile. In my mind, keeping a diary was something girls did.

Thursday, January 11

I've been going back and forth on the idea of this diary. I still feel foolish. But I'm pretty clear that I can't solve this problem on my own. And I'm sure I could never say this face to face to anyone.

Anyway, today I was invited by Ken to go to the mountains for the weekend. Of course, I turned him down. I made up an excuse because I'm afraid to spend that kind of time with anyone, afraid my images might surface and I would be compelled to act on them. Then I would have to find a way to escape. I'm a master at avoiding people. Boy, have I fooled everyone. They think I have a great life, free and easy. No responsibilities. What they don't know is just how piss-assed frightened I really am. Getting too close to anyone means risking discovery. I'd rather blow my brains out than have anyone know.

Saturday, January 13

I awoke this morning as I usually do on Saturdays, feeling a certain calmness. But it's a deceptive calmness. What's really going on is that I'm assured I can do my cruising without the conflict over it interfering with work. Actually, the obsessiveness feels no different at all, except for maybe the fact that I feel less guilty about wasting my time.

So, I spent my afternoon as I usually do, searching for sex. It's so fucking (excuse the pun) easy to find. After so many years, I'm an expert at reading "yes" in their eyes. I can't remember the last time I was turned down, and I never, ever pay for sex. Sounds arrogant and egotistical, but the truth is that it's pathetic. I'd rather be normal.

I listen to other men talk about how often they get rejected. It's ironic this cursed talent I have for finding sexual partners. Of course, most men I know are looking for more than sex. They want to make a connection with another person. I'm exactly the opposite. The last thing I want is to connect. I don't want to know the name of the person I fuck. Most of them don't want to know my name either.

Occasionally, I wonder what it would be like to be in love. I've had friends who were in love, and I've seen what people call love on TV and in the movies. Books, too. I really think my parents love each other. But I haven't a clue about how it would feel. I try not to think too much about it because it makes me feel even more like a freak. From the time I was fifteen, I knew

I wasn't like other guys. They all wanted girlfriends. Sure, they pretended all they wanted was to get fucked, but you could see through their pretenses. They cared and they wanted to be liked. I never felt that way. At fifteen, I was obsessed with scoring. Once I had fucked a girl, I was through with her. Soon, it didn't even matter if it was a girl. I think back on how stupid all the guys were. They thought I was some sort of stud. Of course, they never knew about the guys I fucked. It seemed like a fun game at first, but before I knew it I was out of control. Most of those guys are married now and most still think I'm a stud. What a fucking joke that is.

I'm still not sure why I'm writing all this down. Probably, it's a waste of time.

Monday, January 15

I made a promise to myself that I would get through the week without cruising. I've done it before. Of course, it never lasts long. Can I do it this time?

Friday, January 19

I've been a good boy this week. Instead of screwing around, I focused on work and closed a deal with a major hotel chain. This is the kind of score I really ought to be after. The commission will be enough to get me by for months. Of course, if I could concentrate on work like I did this week, I would really be success-ful. Being successful is everything to me. You couldn't tell that by the way I spend my time. I get in my own fucking way of really achieving something great. Dad didn't let anything get in his way. When he came here he didn't speak a word of English. He worked in a bakery and saved his money. He and Mom still talk about how proud they were the day they bought their first bakery. He turned that one bakery into a gold mine, opening one after another.

It sounds lame but I respect my parents. They're good, kind people. I admire my father for his determination and strong will to succeed. He wanted all three of us to have a college education, and he made sure we got it. My admiration for him far outweighs the times I've been angry with him for being drunk or violent. It didn't happen all that often, and me and my brothers managed to stay out of his way. By the time I was fourteen, I was bigger and stronger than him. He came at me once and I put my fists up to challenge him. He backed down and never laid a hand on me again. Mom has always stayed out of his way in the sense that she stays in the background. But she gets what she wants. She just gets it by being sneaky. When Dad's not around, we sometimes sit and laugh at how all of us can manipulate him. We each have our own tricks.

I'd like to be more like Dad. If I just wasn't obsessive with these thoughts, I know I could be as productive as he is. He's always working, always accomplishing. I waste valuable time with these thoughts. This week I've been great. But tomorrow is Saturday. If I could just get through a Saturday, I think I could conquer this thing.

Saturday, January 20

I woke up thinking about sex. Until I started keeping this diary, I didn't realize how programmed I am. I mean, I certainly knew that sex was on my mind all the time, but this morning I realized that I was actually looking forward to Saturday. I know exactly what I'm going to be doing. I never make plans with anyone because they might interfere. Today's going to be different. I'm going to call Ken and see what he's doing. It's a sure thing if I have the entire day with nothing planned, I'll end up cruising and fucking.

Sunday, January 21

I'm glad I called Ken. We went to the movies. It's been so long since I did anything with another person besides fucking. In fact, I can't remember a Saturday I didn't go cruising and score. This is the best I've felt in a really long time. Maybe it's just keeping this diary that's made a difference. (I still feel foolish.) I'm optimistic I'm going to have another great week. If I could close another sale like last week, I'd feel really great. There's money to be made in selling wine, especially if you can get hotel and restaurant chains. Dad's connections got me started, but I've got to follow through. I could be so rich if I didn't waste so much time searching, always searching. Damn! I want to be rid of this plague.

Sunday, February 25

I quit writing for a while. I thought it was helping, but, as always, I didn't keep my promises to myself. I've been out of control as much this last month as ever. I bet I've had at least twelve partners this month. I don't really count because I don't want to know. It's bound to catch up with me someday. Someone will find out. I worry about being caught all the time, but my worries only seem to make me more out of control. Worrying about being caught is my middle name.

I'm not sure why I'm writing again. I originally thought I might seek some help and that these notes would be useful. But I don't think I could ever let anyone see them. What's the use anyway?

Thursday, March 15

One of my worst fears came true today. I was in fast-food restaurant, having just made a score. We were about to leave together and one of the guys from the office came in. He walked over to the table to say hello. Somehow I felt sure he knew what I was doing. All he did was to make small talk and finally leave. But I didn't introduce him to the woman I was with. How could I? I couldn't remember her name myself. I'm not sure if he figured it out, but if he did, I'm sure he'll blab about it. I've got to get some control over this. I can't keep taking these chances and expect to get away with it.

Friday, March 23

Another week like all the others. Nothing's changed. This week I had sex with two women and one man. I've been thinking again about writing to that sex therapist in the newspaper. Thinking isn't doing.

Sunday, March 25

I decided not to write to the therapist. Instead, I picked up a book I had read about called *Out of the Shadows: Understanding Sexual Addiction*. It was one of the hardest things I've ever done. The joke is that I spend a good part of my waking life in bookstores looking *for* sex. So, it should have been easy for me to go into a bookstore and look for a book *on* sex. Wrong. I was scared shitless someone would notice. And the whole time I was in the store I was feeling the urge. It was so fucking strong that as soon as I left the one bookstore, I was driving to a different kind of bookstore.

Monday, March 26

I read the first part of the book this evening and found myself on almost every page. The guy who wrote it, a Dr. Carnes, says he works with lots of people like me. It's never occurred to me that there are lots of other people like me. It seems silly that I thought this, considering how easy I've found it is to score. Obviously, I'm scoring with other sexaholics.

He thinks sexual addiction is like all other addictions. He says the addict is really substituting a sick relationship for a healthy one. He's got that right. It would be great to be able to have a normal sexual relationship rather than the kind I have. I don't get any kicks from the orgasm. And as soon as I'm done coming, I *have* to get the hell out of there. I don't want to stay around even for a minute.

What scares me the most, though, is the thought that I'd have to give up sex altogether, like an alcoholic has to stay totally away from booze. I don't like the idea. Besides, I don't think I could do it. I think I'd go into a withdrawal, like I do when I try to force myself not to act on my urges. The longer I put it off, the stronger the urge seems, until I feel like I'm going to explode. Then I'm out of control.

I'd like to have a normal sexual relationship, but the idea of no sex at all scares me shitless. It just occurred to me that that may be the reason I've avoided getting any help.

There was one part of the book where I felt this Carnes guy had actually visited the inside of my head. It was the part where he talked about the addiction cycle. He says it starts with a preoccupation which he likens to a trance or mood where you become so absorbed with thoughts of sex you can't get rid of them. That's exactly what happens to me. I get an image of me attracting a target. I do it with my eyes and my body movements. I'm very subtle, but very effective. As soon as the image enters my mind, I can feel myself getting hard. Then I just know I have to act on my arousal or I'll explode.

Then I do exactly what he describes next, the ritualization. That's the routine each addict is supposed to have. For me, that's the part where I end up in an adult bookstore or fast-food place where I know I can score. He claims the ritual actually adds to the arousal and excitement, and I can tell you he's right. I can feel myself getting more and more turned on as I get closer to getting the "target" to say yes.

Next comes the compulsive sexual behavior, which is the actual sex act. According to him it's the end goal of the preoccupation. This is the part I don't actually understand. If it's so important for me to have sex, how come I find so little satisfaction in the act itself? Maybe he explains this later in the book.

Then last, but certainly not least, he talks about feelings of despair. Like I said, I think this guy has been inside my head because I feel like shit afterward. When I'm done, I just want to get the hell out of there. Then, once I'm in the car, I feel ashamed about being powerless to control myself. Starting with the moment the thoughts and images enter my head, I'm in a kind of a trance. I feel like that man in *The Manchurian Candidate* who had a transistorlike gadget inserted in his head that was being controlled by someone else. Once the images start, I feel a rush of adrenaline, and then I know I have to carry out the ritual. It's only after I'm done that I sort of "wake up," as I call it. That's when I feel really rotten. I make promises to myself that I'll never do it again, but I can't help myself. At the most, I've gone two weeks without sex.

Saturday, March 31

I was hoping that reading the book would help me get some control. It hasn't changed a thing. This week I had sex with four different people. I can't even remember what they looked like. They're all a blur. I've got to be beyond help. I don't feel like reading that stupid book anymore. What's the use.

Sunday, April 22

Well, I've taken several weeks' vacation from even thinking about trying to change things. But I feel so empty, so alone. I'll always be alone if I can't get some control over this obsessional behavior of mine. No one would want me the way I am, and there would be no way to keep it a secret. It's too much a part of my life.

So, I've gone back to reading the book. One part of it really does describe me. He talks about the addict living in constant personal "jeopardy." More than anything else he's said, I can relate to that. I live my life hiding from people, fearful they will unmask my secret life. Secrecy is what I am about. It guides everything I do.

In fact, as I write these words, a part of me is thinking I will somehow share them with someone who can help me. But there's another part of me that's convinced I won't ever be able to show this to anyone. I haven't stopped feeling foolish about writing all this down.

Monday, April 23

I was reading in Dr. Carnes's book about one of the cases he describes. It was about a boy who was sexually aroused by a priest during confessional. When I read this I got very angry. I threw the book across the room and started pacing. I felt a pain inside me that I've never felt before and a feeling that I wanted to scream. But I didn't. It took me more than an hour to calm down.

Later that night, just as I was falling asleep, a strong image came to me. It was an image of me when I was around ten years old. I know this because it was during the time I was an altar boy. I used to go to the rectory to visit this one priest. He was popular with all the boys because he was quite different. He used to drive a motorcycle and sometimes took us for rides. The image was of being in the rectory alone with him on a Saturday. Then the image became a vivid memory. He pulled out a porn magazine and showed me some of the pictures. Then he asked me if I liked looking at the pictures. I must have gotten an erection because I remember him reaching down and touching my cock and saying something like "Boy, that's a good one." It scared the shit out of me, and I ran like hell out of there. I never went back, and after that I must have lost interest in being an altar boy. I never even considered telling my parents. I didn't think they would believe me. And besides, you didn't talk about anything like that around them.

Interesting, though. This memory now connects me to another memory. It was shortly after the incident with the priest that I started collecting pornographic magazines. I used them to masturbate to. Now, one more memory comes to mind. I found a box of these magazines out in the alley, apparently left as trash. I took the box home but didn't know where I could keep them. All I knew was that I didn't want Mom to find out. You couldn't talk about anything sexual with Mom. If she found the magazines, she'd throw a fit. I'm not sure what Dad would have done, but we never once talked about anything sexual either.

Anyway, I remember wrapping the box in one of

those big trash bags and hiding it in the backyard bushes of one of the neighbors. I'd sneak out at times, being very careful not to get caught, and get one of the magazines. It would always be when Mom wasn't home. Still, I worried the whole time she might come home and catch me. I can't even remember how it all ended and whatever happened to all those magazines. Seems strange to me that I can remember finding and hiding the magazines, but I can't remember what I did with them. Anyway, I vividly remember living in constant fear of being caught even though I never was.

As I wrote the previous words, it occurred to me that the fear of being caught back then is very much like the fear I have now of being caught. Obviously, there must be some connection. Which brings me once again to wonder if this sex therapist could make any sense of the connection.

Sunday, April 29

I can't explain it but I didn't even feel like cruising this week. The images never came to mind.

Something else did cross my mind, however. I finished reading Dr. Carnes's book. He talks about the importance of joining a group for sexaholics. He claims it's the best way to lick the addiction. All I could think about is how tempting it would be to be in a room with all these people who are obsessed by sex.

Sunday, May 6

Another week went by and I didn't go out searching. Something's changing for me. I don't know what it is. I don't care. It's been two weeks and I haven't had sex. I feel great. Maybe just reading the book helped. I'm not going to analyze it.

Sunday, May 20

I just looked at my last entry. I guess I was feeling optimistic when I last wrote. It didn't last. I've lost count of the number of partners I've had since that Sunday. Except for yesterday, it's the same thing all over again. But yesterday I had another one of those rare experiences where I felt something for the person I was with. Usually, I avoid approaching attractive women or men because they fall for me. I despise attachments and hate conversation so I don't want my target to care. Since I know where to look, it's pretty easy to find another person who doesn't care much about talking either. I can tell simply by looking into their eyes that they want what I want. But this woman yesterday was different. She was attractive and I found that I did enjoy talking to her. We spent several hours talking and eventually ended up in bed, but the whole experience was unusual for me. I enjoyed her touch and felt like we had some mutual appreciation. What wasn't different was that after the sex was over, I still felt that familiar need to leave. I didn't even notice her last name, so I know I won't see her again. This feeling has happened maybe half a dozen times in the past. I don't understand it. I used to think it meant I was making progress in kicking the addiction. But not anymore.

Saturday, May 26

I've had a good week, but today will be the test. I'm going to wash my car and go grocery shopping. Tonight I'm going over to my parents' for dinner. I haven't seen them in a while, and I miss sitting around the table and joking with them.

God, if they ever found out about this double life I lead, it would break their hearts. Mom is so embarrassed by anything sexual. If something remotely sexual comes on TV, she gets up and leaves or turns to another station. She's always been like that. I'm lucky she never discovered any of those magazines I used to keep hidden. She would never have forgiven me. The only thing I ever remember her saying about sex was that it was ''something sacred between a husband and a wife.'' Sometimes it's hard to believe that I'm her son. The last thing sex is to me is sacred.

Sunday, May 27

It was good to see Mom and Dad again, although the wear and tear of Dad's hectic life does finally seem to be showing on him. He looked tired.

Yesterday, I reread Dr. Carnes's book. But I still don't get it. He talks about disorders within the family as being responsible for distorting a child's thinking. If that applies in my case, I don't know why. All I feel from my parents is love. If anything, they were a little overprotective, certainly not punishing or abusive. He says all addicts believe that no one would love them as they are and that they use sex as a substitute for the intimacy they crave, but are afraid will be denied them.

If I'm honest, I have to admit that I question whether my parents would still love me if they found out about my sexual behavior. But I just don't remember feeling unloved or lonely as a child. Even the few times Dad lost control and hit me, I knew it was because he wasn't himself when he had too much to drink. But it was rare that he would lose control. Mom was too afraid to do much of anything when he was that out of control. Everybody was afraid. I wonder if I'm just trying to make excuses for him. Perhaps this is a question a therapist could answer. I still haven't ruled out completely the idea of seeing a therapist. But I can't see myself looking somebody in the eye and saying the things I'm writing about.

Saturday, June 2

Every gain I've made was lost today. When I woke this morning, I planned out my entire day so I wouldn't have time to go searching. But it didn't turn out that way. By two o'clock this afternoon I was in the bookstore, by two-thirty I was in bed fucking. By three o'clock I was back in my car and headed for home. For the first time ever, I thought about just driving my car into a concrete embankment and ending it all. It all seems so hopeless.

I was feeling so guilty and humiliated by the time I got home, I called information and got the phone number of the Sexaholics Anonymous chapter closest to me. Dr. Carnes thinks this is the only way an addict can gain any control. He believes in a Twelve-Step program similar to Alcoholics Anonymous. Could I really be in a room with other sex addicts? It seems to me I would go crazy trying to decide which one I wanted to fuck. And yet, who I fuck really seems to make little difference.

I'm feeling desperate. Am I desperate enough to try something as risky as joining a group of crazy addicts like myself?

Sunday, June 10

I had a terrible week. I couldn't concentrate on work and spent time driving aimlessly around. All I managed to do was postpone by several hours picking someone up. Eventually, however, I did what I always do.

So, Saturday night I actually went to an SA meeting. It was bizarre. I'm glad I didn't have to say a thing because my voice would have shaken as badly as my knees were shaking. Guys were actually standing up and talking about it. I don't think I could ever tell another person, let alone a group of people, about my problem.

Yet, there was a guy there talking about being arrested for exposing himself in public. And there was another guy who told about how he constantly has to dress in women's clothes and go searching for sex. One guy had been in prison twice for having sex with young boys. He was in his fifties and talking about how, even after years of prison, he still has the desire. Jesus, it was scary.

The one thing that was very interesting was that everyone seemed to believe that, like me, they first get an image in their head and that the image drives them toward the behavior. It was fascinating for me to hear other men talk about getting an image. I've always thought that something had gone wrong with me, something in my genes had gone haywire and caused my brain to think strangely. But after listening to these men talk, I'm not sure anymore. Could all of us have had the same thing go wrong?

Until tonight, I never realized how convinced I was that I was somehow defective. I mean, ever since I started being obsessed with these images at around age fifteen, I've felt different from other guys. And I've always known that being secretive was essential—so essential that I knew I would have to kill myself if I was ever discovered. Now I realize the images started after I stopped using the magazines to masturbate to.

These two things, the images and the secretiveness, have always made me different. But it was only tonight, while I was listening to these other men talk, that I finally was able to understand what I've believed all along that I was born with this problem. A mutation of the genes or something.

But then these men started talking about some of their early experiences with sex. What really surprised me was the similarities around the issue of guilt. I mean, I remember vividly how I was so worried that I might get caught with those magazines. The fear created an adrenaline rush, which only heightened the sexual arousal I felt. I heard the same kind of story from these men. They all mentioned having some sort of physical high as a result of the fear of being caught. The fear doesn't stop them but spurs them on to commit whatever perverted sexual act they're addicted to. What I don't understand is why the fear doesn't keep us from acting on the images. Isn't fear supposed to keep you from doing things?

On the way out of the meeting, this man walked up to me, acting very friendly. He acknowledged that I must be new because he hadn't seen me before. He introduced himself but, of course, I can't remember his name. I've gotten to be an expert at forgetting names. Anyway, I thought maybe he was trying to pick me up so I wasn't too friendly. I was thinking how I needed this group to help me, not to provide a convenient stable of sex partners.

He must have been reading my mind because he came right out and said he wasn't trying to score. Just to be friendly. He asked me to join him for coffee. Reluctantly, I decided I'd go. He talked a lot about his problem. He said he's been married for fifteen years but can't stop thinking about women with perfect bodies. He said he evaluates the body of every woman he sees. It is such a preoccupation that it interferes with his work.

I guess he was expecting me to tell him about why I was attending an SA meeting, but I kept quiet. I'm not telling anybody. When I didn't say much about myself, he went on to tell me about an experience he had when he was about twelve. He said his parents owned this apartment building and there was this tenant in it that took pornographic pictures for a living. The tenant brought him inside the apartment and showed him hundreds of pictures of women that were all over the walls of the apartment.

He remembered getting aroused, but at the same time he felt very afraid because he thought he might get caught. He claimed his parents were very strict and prudish, and he knew if he got caught, he would be in big trouble. He told me about being punished once in high school for walking a girl home.

Then he told me how he had really wanted to stay and look at the pictures and enjoy the pleasant feeling of being aroused. Instead, he ran out of the apartment. He didn't want to go home because his parents always quizzed him about where he was and what he was doing. But the longer he stayed away from home, the worse the inquisition would be. He didn't have any choice. When he got home, his mom, as predicted, asked him where he had been. He got panicky, so he lied.

While I was driving home, I started thinking about what this man had told me. Again, the similarity of fear being associated with getting turned on came to my mind. I know there is an important connection here, but I'm too tired to think about it anymore. I've never written so much at one time, but then I've never experienced anything like tonight. It's curiosity that would get me back to another meeting.

Sunday, June 17

I had an incredibly good week. The images left me alone all week. At first I thought about not going back to the SA meeting, but I've finally accepted that one week without this obsession means nothing.

I decided to try SA one more time. I wasn't quite as nervous this week as I was last time. And the guy I went for coffee with was there. This time I made sure I remembered his name: Bill. The format of the meeting

was the same. In the beginning of the meeting someone read the Twelve Steps. Then guys just stood up
and talked about their particular problems. Others
would be supportive or sometimes challenging when
they thought they were hearing bullshit.

Bill came up to me at the end of the meeting and
asked if I had found a sponsor. I knew from reading
Dr. Carnes's book that a sponsor is supposed to be
your connection to the group, a person to always be
there for you while you work through the Steps. But I
wasn't sure I even wanted to work through the Steps.
The First Step requires talking out loud about your
problem. I had never talked to anyone about it, and I
wasn't sure I ever could. I told Bill I'd think about it.

And I have. But I just can't get a picture in my head
of me standing up in front of a group of people admitting that I'm obsessed about finding meaningless sex.
Others have said the same thing, but that's them, not
me. I'm just not sure if this group is the right place for
me.

Wednesday, June 20

I went to dinner at my parents' tonight. Mom asked if
I was dating anyone. This conversation occurs every
few months. I know she's just concerned about me, but
I hate it when she brings up the subject. At these times,
I really believe she suspects something's not right. It
makes me so nervous when they bring up the subject.
I hate their questions, and often I lie about some girl
that I was dating and then make up some cock-and-
bull story about why it didn't work out. They probably
know I'm lying but don't force the issue because
they're afraid their worst suspicions might be true: that
I'm gay.

The truth is I don't know what I am. When I want a
sexual partner, it doesn't seem to matter whether it's a

man or a woman. Who they are has never mattered. Just like the orgasm itself really doesn't matter, although I feel driven to have one. I always feel empty inside immediately after I come. What I really feel is worse than empty. What I really feel is hard to describe.

I don't think I'm gay. What I am or what I've got can't be put in a category like that. It's more complicated, more confusing, more undefined. I think I'd rather have them believe I'm gay than to know the truth. I couldn't live with their knowing what I'm really like.

I'm beginning to get those feelings again that I should call that therapist. I wanted to ask Bill if therapists think sex addicts should be castrated or something similar, but I just couldn't talk about it with him.

Thinking about the sex therapist made me think about the article she wrote on sexual addiction, so I pulled it out of its hiding place and read it again. It made more sense now that I've listened to other people like myself tell their stories.

She says compulsive sexual behavior comes from a distortion in the developmental sexual process. What a mouthful! She talks about certain periods in a child's sexual development in which he or she is vulnerable to things going astray. If I understand her correctly, she believes that when normal sexual feelings are made to feel abnormal, the feelings get attached to fantasies and practices that are considered abnormal and, therefore, socially forbidden.

The example she gave helped me to understand what she was saying, and it sure fit many of the stories I heard at SA. She told the story of a boy about eight years old who remembered getting aroused while peeping through the door of his older sister's room when she was getting dressed. He was confused by these new feelings but remembered how good it felt. His mother caught him and punished him by spanking him, verbally admonishing him, and sending him to his room. He was just a kid who got turned on by looking at his sister, but he was made to feel guilty about it. According to her, a flaw in the developmental process was unintentionally, but nevertheless destructively, created. This boy grew up to be a Peeping Tom, his sexual arousal dependent on the combination of fear of being caught and guilt over being aroused. For him, sexual arousal under normal circumstances was impossible. Being with a woman who wanted to be with him lacked the fear and guilt that he required for arousal.

When I read this article before, I guess I wasn't really ready to understand it because now I see myself in her descriptions. Maybe listening to those other men helped me to see more clearly what I've been doing. I just this minute realized that I've made the same connection as the boy in the story. The fear of being caught is essential to my arousal. That's why I don't give a damn who my partner is.

It has to have something to do with those magazines and the fear of being caught. And maybe even that incident with that priest was the beginning. It just never occurred to me that one experience could be so crucial. I'd forgotten all about the incident with the priest.

So, now what? Will any of these brilliant insights make a damn bit of difference? Will they free me of this obsession? Bill says you're never free of your addiction, you only learn how to control it. Is he right? Or can this sex therapist help free me so I can be normal? I'll never know the answer to that unless I tell on myself. But do I have the guts?

I finished reading the diary, and as I put the papers aside, I noticed that I did so with a loud sigh. It was a sigh of ironic frustration: another innocent victim of a culture that so fears sexual urges it creates the very distortions it fears. Another self-fulfilling prophecy: a child whose normal sexual urges were made to feel abnormal, so that he ended up acting out his feelings in abnormal ways.

The man whose story I had just read was describing a condition known as *paraphilia*. The word comes from two Greek roots, *philia*, meaning "love," and *para*, meaning "beyond what is ordinary," i.e., abnormal. Paraphilia takes on a wide variety of forms, from compulsive cruising, to exhibitionism, to child molestation, to rape, to many other behaviors that the general public rarely hears about. The one common element in all paraphilics is their obsessive-compulsive nature; paraphilics feel unable to control their behavior. Because of this aspect, their behavior has been labeled by some sexologists as "addictive."

What I read was not surprising to me. I've heard it in many forms before. Nor was it surprising to me that this patient had sought out Dr. Carnes's book. Except for the fact that most are male, paraphilics cannot be stereotyped into a class or type of person. Because it's less threatening, most of us think of sexual addicts as degenerates. The truth is that the majority are bright people, normal in every other way except for their paraphilia. They are people who live next door and work alongside all of us. That is exactly why, when you read about some strange sexual tragedy in the newspaper, neighbors are always quoted as saying that he or she was such a nice, quiet person—the least likely suspect in such a horrible tragedy.

As an example of how "normal-"appearing and intelligent a paraphilic can be, I am reminded of a patient, a young attorney, who was addicted to autoerotic asphyxiation. That's where a person uses a scarf, pantyhose, or other similar material to cut off his air supply while he masturbates to orgasm. The lack of oxygen supposedly heightens the orgasm. It's a delicate balancing act of reaching orgasm before the lack of oxygen is irreversible. Unfortunately, as many police- and firemen will tell you, some end by killing themselves.

This patient showed up at my office immaculately dressed in corporate attire: dark gray suit, white button-down shirt, and maroon tie. From his briefcase he handed me a stack of papers, two articles from the psychiatric literature and two from police literature on the subject of autoerotic asphyxiation. He had obviously done quite a bit of homework on his compulsive behavior. Unfortunately, he was in my office not because he wanted to stop the behavior, but because his wife was threatening him with divorce if he didn't seek treatment. He came for only the one visit and didn't show up for his next appointment.

This, too, is quite common. People who exhibit compulsive sexual behavior rarely seek voluntary psychiatric treatment. Usually they are sent by the courts or seek help because they've been threatened with abandonment by their families. Like the man whose diary I had just finished reading, most are afraid that treatment means having to give up sex altogether. The idea of life without sex is inconceivable. Most voluntary patients quit treatment shortly after starting.

In this way, sexual compulsivity does resemble other, more familiar, addictions such as those to alcohol or food. For the few who do actually seek treatment, starting and stopping is a part of the cycle of addiction, the familiar revolving-door phenomenon. Promises to stop, such as the ones described in the diary above, are made and broken thousands of times. As with other addictions, compulsive sexual behavior is almost always imbued with some degree of secretiveness, scheming, and deceit. At the same time it is brazen and self-incriminating.

For example, the young attorney I mentioned above would sometimes disappear for twenty-four hours. He would check into a hotel room where he could, in private, repeatedly engage in his compulsive behavior. Yet, when asked to account for his absence by his wife and co-workers, he would make up obviously contradictory stories. Eventually, his careless lying caused his wife to follow him to the hotel. Just like the attorney, the diarist was obsessive about secrecy and yet was blatantly public about his cruising.

It is most important to understand, however, that compulsive sexual behavior is extremely particular. That is, the paraphilic is addicted to something sexually specific, not just *anything* sexual. So, the man who sent me his diary is addicted to indiscriminate cruising, seeking sex with a plurality of partners. The young attorney is addicted to autoerotic asphyxiation, and the Peeping Tom I mentioned in my newspaper article is addicted to voyeuristic pleasure. Paraphilics do not cross over the boundaries of their own particular addictions. I had a patient once who was addicted to erotic words. This is known as *narratophilia*. He insisted that his wife tell him erotic stories prior to each sexual encounter. At first she thought it was just a game but eventually learned that it was mandatory for his arousal. He became aggressive and threatening if she refused. Narratophilia is quite distinctive from *pictophilia*, which is addiction to erotic pictures.

It is precisely this fact, that addictions are sexually specific, that helps us to understand the origins of compulsive sexual behaviors. All of the above individuals initially encountered a negative experience that was linked with a pleasant erotic experience. The man who sent me his diary described how he was turned on by the material the priest showed to him, yet was terribly frightened of being caught. Bill, the addict he met at SA, had the similar experience when he visited the apartment of the man who took the pornographic photographs. The Peeping Tom was caught and punished for sneaking a look at his naked sister. And, as it turned out, the young attorney told me how, as a young child, he used to get badly beaten by his father and sent to his room. While alone in his room, he would administer further punishment to himself for being a "bad" boy. The punishment would consist of tying himself up for hours. As he got older, he discovered masturbation. He also discovered he could heighten his punishment for being "bad" by challenging his life: suffocation first or orgasm first.

Becoming addicted to something that was originally very negative is not as unusual as you might first think. I saw a movie once about a rock climber who had been practicing his sport for more than thirteen years. He mentioned that his major motivation was "his fear of heights." In fact, most daredevils, like most sexual addicts, are motivated by the adrenaline rush they get from the experience of fear. It's quite possible that the adrenaline actually imprints or changes the brain in some way. Recent research is looking into the possibility of chemical changes that occur in the brain as a result of the euphoria that comes from transcending fear.

The biology and physiology of how sexuality develops remain somewhat of a mystery. But it is clear that these processes are more complex than can be observed from outside the human body. At birth, a child's brain is not yet fully developed. Hormones, which are never dormant, continue, at programmed intervals, to influence future sexual motivations and behavior.

Studies of animals have shown that normal sexual rehearsal play in childhood is essential to adult sexual functioning. In childhood, animals deprived of the opportunity to mimic adult heterosexual behavior will not mate as adults, their pair-bonding ability having been damaged. While I believe strongly that we must exercise caution in drawing human inferences from animal studies, my experience with clients whose childhoods involved extreme guilt around normal sexual play indicates to me that fear, deprivation, or excessive disciplining of this play can have serious consequences. In our culture, the sexual rehearsal play of children frightens adults—thus, my earlier comment on how society creates the very distortions it so fears.

Dr. John Money, in his book *Lovemaps*, describes what he thinks is responsible for the distortions that occur in people's sexual attachments:

> The cleft between saintly love and sinful lust is omnipresent in the sexuoerotic heritage of our culture. Love is undefiled and saintly. Lust is defiling and sinful. Love exists above the belt, lust below. Love is lyrical. Lust is lewd. Love is heralded in public. Lust is hidden in private. Love displayed is championed, but championships for lust are condemned. Love is candid and speaks its name. Lust is clandestine and euphemizes its name.
>
> In some degree or another, the cleavage between love and lust gets programmed into the design of the lovemaps of all developing boys and girls. . . . A shared principle of all paraphilic lovemaps is that they represent tragedy turned into triumph. The tragedy is the defacement of an ordinarily developing heterosexual lovemap. The triumph is the rescue of lust from total wreckage and obliteration and its attachment to a redesigned lovemap. The new map gives lust a second chance, but at a price. . . . A paraphilic lovemap is a ruse of sorts—a circuitous or behind-the-scenes way of getting a certificate of admission to the theater of lust.

What Dr. Money is suggesting, and I agree, is that the need for human sexual expression is so strong that it exerts its power over cultural attempts to defile it, even at the expense of distortion. What happens in some extreme situations is a complete splitting of love and lust. Splitting the two means that an individual is unable to feel intimacy and love for the same person for whom he or she feels lust. The man in the diary incorporates lust into his "lovemap" on the condition that the partner be unqualified or ineligible to be a "saint defiled." He accomplishes this by choosing anonymous partners for whom he feels nothing, his prototype for this distortion being the priest (saint) who caused him to have unacceptable lustful feelings.

As in the case of the young attorney, many paraphilics manage to get married, giving the appearance that they have made a successful love-sex bonding. However, when you talk to their mates, you discover that partner sex has always been marginal at best. Usually, the paraphilic is able to "perform" early in the relationship but then becomes masterful at avoiding further intimacy. Or in the case of a fetish, where the addiction is to a certain object, the object must be present for arousal to occur. Because some paraphilics are able to maintain some semblance of normalcy in the beginning of a relationship, some future mates are truly fooled. However, more frequently than not, the future partner uses denial to block out the unpleasant truth.

For example, I'm reminded of a young woman who came to me because she discovered that her fiancé, a promising politician, had been secretly harboring hundreds of pornographic magazines. She had met him nine months earlier and had been engaged to him for about six months, and the wedding was only a month away. She had first discovered the magazines about a month before the engagement. When she confronted him about her discovery, he promised to throw them all away. Two months later, she once again found a large collection of magazines. Again, he promised he would never touch another magazine. In the meantime, partner sex was practically nonexistent, as he was constantly "stressed and under pressure" as a result of one political crisis or another. When she sought me out, she had once again found another cache of magazines. What should she do? she asked.

Suspecting that she had fallen in love with a pictophilic, I told her to postpone the wedding. I suggested there was much about this man she still needed to know. She told me she loved him. Wasn't that what was important? And besides, the invitations to the wedding were already sent. She felt sure that everything would get back to normal, including their sex life, once they were married and once he was out from under some of the political pressure he was feeling. I told her she was fooling herself. She questioned how I could be so certain that he couldn't keep his promise. I explained to her about the problems of sexual addictions. She chose not to listen. Two years later I received a phone call from her. He had ceased hiding, but not using, the magazines, and she hadn't had sex with him in more than a year. She had threatened to leave him, and he had promised "never to touch another magazine." Should she believe him? she asked.

Paraphilia is not a bad habit that can be broken by willpower. As mentioned, there is more and more evidence to indicate that changes in the brain, specifically the hypothalamus, occur during prepubertal sexual development and therefore are extremely resistant to change. The human body is designed to acquire knowledge and skills over time, and there are windows of opportunity for acquiring certain skills. For example, the motor and sensory skills needed to learn to ride a bicycle are maximized at around six years of age. A child learning to ride a bike at that age is likely to be successful within a few hours or less—and once learned the skill is never forgotten. However, as any adult who bypassed this window can tell you, learning to ride a bicycle as an adult can be a difficult to near-impossible task. And those who do learn at a later age will tell you they are never completely comfortable while on a bicycle.

Sexual development has windows of opportunity as well. Childhood and adolescent sexual rehearsal play is essential to normal, heterosexual adult functioning. Playing "doctor" with a neighborhood playmate can be a very healthy experience. Masturbation is also a normal, healthy experience. And getting aroused from viewing erotic scenes, either of real people or in magazines, is not only normal but also can be very healthy. Dating and petting are ways in which adolescents practice and prepare for future love-sex bonding. Without the opportunity to "practice" as a child and adolescent, adults, like the cyclists, are never quite comfortable with their sexuality.

Of course, it's possible for sexual rehearsal to become unhealthy. One of the most important criteria for keeping it healthy is to keep it age-concordant. Two neighborhood children age four playing "doctor" is normal and healthy. A twelve-year-old and a four-year-old playing doctor is not healthy because there is too much difference in power between them. Not only is the twelve-year-old developmentally ahead of the four-year-old, but he or she is also bigger and stronger and can exert power over the younger child. Using power to preexpose a child to sexual experiences he or she is not developmentally ready for creates confusion and distortion of future sexuality—as did the incident (described by the diary keeper) with the priest, a truly powerful and revered man.

As a society, our lack of understanding about what is healthy and unhealthy sexual rehearsal play has resulted in a blanket policy of forbidding all sexual play. As a result, adults who mean to be protective can easily end up being destructive. Bill, the man from SA, is a perfect example. His parents were obviously overprotective. So fearful were they that he might be sexual with a girl, they even forbade him to walk a girl home from school. Unknowingly, they were depriving Bill of important early skills necessary for healthy sex as an adult by instilling guilt where none need be. Guilt around sexual feelings was firmly planted by the time Bill unintentionally experienced arousal from viewing the pornographic pictures in the man's apartment. When you add the circumstances surrounding the viewing—an older, more powerful adult and the clandestine nature of the situation—you create an unhealthy, learned association that is not easily unlearned.

As I mentioned earlier, it seems to be the combination of such powerful emotions as guilt and fear with sexual arousal that results in imprinting the brain. It's the imprinting that makes the resulting abnormal behaviors so resistant to change. The repetitive pattern of rapists, child molesters, Peeping Toms, exhibitionists, compulsive cruisers, and others with abnormal sexual behaviors demonstrates the truth of this statement. Which, of course, brings up the question of the best way to deal with such behaviors.

Within the field of sexology, there are two basic, sometimes overlapping, yet essentially oppositional, camps regarding the issue of treatment. On the one side are those who believe that paraphilia is another form of addiction and should be treated as such. Patrick Carnes, the author of *Out of the Shadows: Understanding Sexual Addiction,* pioneered the idea of using a modified Twelve-Step program of Alcoholics Anonymous (AA) in his work with sexual offenders in prison. He believes that sexual addicts have distortions in their thinking processes that can be reframed into new, more positive, ways of thinking. He believes that, as a result of working in a group, addicts can support one another through the process of change. But he also believes, as do those who endorse the AA philosophy, that recovery is a lifelong process that requires active participation in the Twelve-Step program.

On the other side are those who believe that there is danger in labeling sexual addictions as equal to other addictions. The danger comes in the tendency to simplify what is actually a very complex problem. Lumping all addictions together results in a cultural tendency to treat all addicts alike. It would give our culture a simple, convenient, and inappropriate scapegoat for sexual behaviors that are not understood, but negatively judged. One real danger would be that further brain research on compulsive sexual behaviors would cease to exist. As Domeena C. Renshaw, M.D., director of the Sexual Dysfunction Clinic, Loyola University of Chicago, says: "A Nobel Peace Prize would be most fittingly endowed to those who unlock the scientific code of that segment of the hypothalamus that could alleviate the paraphilic's sexual distress." I agree with Dr. Renshaw and with Dr. Money: There is much more to compulsive sexual behavior than distorted thought processes.

Perhaps there is no better evidence of the complexity of compulsive sexual behavior than the fact that the male is much more vulnerable to it than the female. Female paraphilics are rare, the actual number being difficult to determine because of failure to report the behavior. Dr. Money believes that the greater vulnerability of the male is somehow based on his greater dependence on the visual image for erotic arousal. He believes that with further research it could eventually be shown that males have a greater sensitivity to visual arousal than females and that this sensitivity is determined in utero. He speaks of the importance of imagery to compulsive sexual behavior. According to Dr. Money and every patient who has told me his story, the imagery comes first, and then it gets translated into practice.

If distortions in thinking alone were creating the compulsive behavior, males and females would be equally vulnerable. Especially if, as Dr. Carnes suggests, parental abuse, neglect, and abandonment were responsible for the distortions in thinking. Female children are certainly not exempt from such negative experiences. Dr. Carnes accounts for the large difference between the number of male addicts and female addicts by focusing on the issue of male powerlessness over female seduction. This myth originated with Adam and Eve and has continued until the present time. He says, "If a man comes from a family in which he feels bad about himself, has little confidence women would want to be with him, and believes that sex is the one comfort he cannot do without, addiction can occur. Place that same man in a culture which makes women into sexual objects and addiction will thrive."

Dr. Carnes accurately portrays our culture, but I believe it's not that simple. All men are raised with the belief that women have sexual power over them. All men do not become addicts. And, more importantly, remember that addictions are very specific and *are not addictions to sex with women*. The man who sent me his diary is addicted to the adrenaline rush he gets from the secretiveness of his search and the anonymity of his partner. He doesn't even care if his target is male or female. Bill, the man from SA, is addicted to the *image* of the perfect female body, not to sex with the perfect body. The politician is addicted to pictures in magazines; the last thing he is interested in is a real, live woman.

So, what is the most appropriate way to deal with compulsive sexual behavior? Will groups like SA solve the problem? Or is further research into the chemistry of the brain needed? And what about the use of standard psychotherapy? These are all questions that need answering. Individual testimonies of people who have been helped by groups such as SA cannot be ignored. There is a desperate need for such groups.

The danger in labels such as "sexual addiction" is that it offers a convenient scapegoat for lack of parental and societal responsibility in the development of healthy sexuality in our children. If society and parents blame the adult by lumping him or her into a category called addict, it camouflages their contribution to the problem. Searching for a simplistic label for behaviors we abhor but do not understand leads to a dead end. Research—not labels—is what is needed.

Chemical treatment of compulsive sexual behavior is still in its infancy. In 1978, Dr. John Money, whom I referred to above, founded the Johns Hopkins Biosexual Psychohormonal Clinic for the treatment of paraphilic sex-offending and related disorders. His clinic is experimenting with the use of progesterone and its synthetic relatives. Early evidence indicates that these drugs act as sexuoerotic tranquilizers. Contrary to popular belief, paraphilics do not have higher than normal levels of testosterone. Yet, by using drugs that lower the levels of testosterone in men with this disorder, their behaviors become more controllable.

Money has had some promising results with paraphilics who do not threaten the safety of others, such as asphyxiophilics and compulsive masturbators. Prior to treatment, preoccupation with imagery is unrelenting and may entail as many as six to ten ejaculations a day, either by masturbation or with a partner, or both. Drug treatment can significantly reduce the preoccupation so that a person may lead a more normal existence. However, successful outcome of hormonal treatment for the more aggressive paraphilics, such as rapists and child molesters, is still pending because society insists on prison rather than what is still experimental treatment for such known individuals. The successful outcome of hormonal treatment has to be tested in real life; prison in no way mimics real life.

In short, there is much we still do not know about what causes compulsive sexual behavior. Further exploration and research are desperately needed. Psychotherapy alone is rarely effective in deterring the behavior. Yet, psychotherapy is extremely beneficial in helping the tormented individual deal with feelings of being freakish and alone in a world that is totally misunderstanding, punitive, and rejecting. The best results have been attained from a combination of chemical and talking therapy, whether group therapy, individual therapy, or a combination of the two.

Since my private practice is not associated with the courts, I have not had in treatment any paraphilics who would be considered dangerous to someone other than themselves. Very few sex offenders seek voluntary treatment. Compulsive cruisers, who never pay for sex, break no laws and are therefore not considered sex offenders. However, with the advent of AIDS, compulsive cruising no longer can be seen as a victimless act. The man whose diary I just finished reading mentioned only once that he was risking his life. Until I meet him, I can only speculate that he is in denial of just how dangerous and lethal he might be to others.

At his appointed time, the man who sent his diary arrived in my office. The name he gave me was Greg, and, as I had suspected, his appearance in no way reflected the specific distortions going on in his head. He was dressed in dark slacks, white dress shirt, and maroon tie. He was a slim, youthful thirty-two-year-old, and, as alluded to in his diary, he worked as a salesman for a distributor of fine wines. College-educated and quite articulate, he had the character-istic dark, Apollo-like features of his Greek ancestry. His manner was subdued, almost arrogant in its gentility. Had I not read his diary, I would not have initially known that underneath his facade was a confused, angry, and very dis-traught man.

He spoke softly and chose his words carefully.

"As I mentioned in my . . . diary—I'm still uncomfort-able with that word but don't know what else to call it."

"Why not call it your story?"

"Yes, that's better. Well, in my story, I mentioned how difficult this meeting would be for me. And it is. Very."

"You don't show it."

"Ah, well, that's because I'm quite a master of deceit. Deceit is an avocation for someone like me."

"Yes, the fear of discovery is what it's all about. From what I read, I think you now understand the whole thing started with a fear of discovery."

"I understand what you said in that newspaper article, but I'm not sure I believe it. It seems almost impossible to me that one incident could cause such damage."

"Don't forget, the theme was repeated over and over again with the pornographic magazines. Fear of discovery was a part of each and every one of those incidents as well. And there may have been some earlier incidents, when you were much younger, that you may not remember."

"What do you mean?"

"Well, if you had a crystal ball that could take you far enough back into the history of most people with compulsive sexual behavior, you would usually discover earlier instances of anxiety around sexual feelings. Maybe being caught masturbating or playing 'doctor,' for example. And it may not even be a particular incident but more of an atmosphere in the home that sexual feelings are taboo."

"That certainly describes my home. My mother is very religious. 'Sex' was a word that was never spoken in our home when she was around. Yet I know my father is a very sexual man."

"How do you know that?"

"He was always after my mother. You know, pinching her on the butt and stuff. It was kind of silly because we knew what was going on, but Mom insisted it be so secretive. She was always hushing Dad and saying the kids might hear."

"So, she was afraid she might be discovered?"

"I see what you're getting at. You're saying I was set up."

"Not intentionally. It's just that when parents are so secretive about sex, they pass on a message that sex is not okay. Secrets are kept because of shameful feelings. So, if sex is secretive, children learn it's something to be ashamed about."

"It's not that I don't understand what you're saying. But I still can't comprehend that it could get so off track. I mean, if my parents had beaten me or been really mean to me like some of the men in the SA group talked about—well, then I could understand how it could screw up a kid's mind. But my parents loved me, and, except for a very few times, never even hit me."

"It's true, Greg, that we don't understand completely how sexual thoughts can get so off track. But we do know that strong feelings of guilt or shame around childhood sexual impulses interfere with the normal developmental process."

He gave me a very pleasant smile and said, "You like that phrase, don't you?"

"Yes, I guess I do."

Returning to his more serious manner, he asked, "So, what's in store for me? Can you help me to change? I mean, will I ever be able to fall in love like other people?"

I knew the question would come eventually. Still, I'm always uncomfortable when it's asked because I can't give an unequivocal answer. "I don't know if the damage that's been done is repairable or not. Other people with problems like yours have success stories to tell. But it never seems to happen easily. You're doing all the right things. Support groups and psychotherapy are a beginning. And, if you want, I'll put you in contact with research centers that use medication to help control this type of problem."

"Will I have to give up sex altogether? Sex has been a preoccupation of mine for so long that I'm not sure I'd even know what to do or think about if I wasn't thinking about sex."

"You're right. To keep from feeling a terrible void, you'd have to find other interests. But I don't want to make it sound like the solution is as simple as finding a hobby to entertain you. The imagery you experience isn't under your control. What you end up doing about the imagery may be something you *can* control.

"And, Greg, I know you're aware that you're risking your life and the lives of others by having so many partners."

"Yes, I know. But the most I've been able to do is stay away from sex for a few weeks. Then the compulsion finally gets to me and I have to do it. I'm weak when it comes to sex."

"Well, that's a place we can start in therapy. It's not a weakness. It's a flaw in your developmental process which creates the images."

My last remark got the smile I hoped it would.

Greg returned for three more sessions. With each session he became increasingly concerned about whether he would have to give up sex altogether. Additionally, he admitted to expectations that therapy would create immediate and dramatic results in his behavior. But nothing was changing.

I could see that I was losing him to his feelings of failure. I talked to him about his unrealistic expectations, but I could tell he wasn't really absorbing what I was saying. And then there was the issue of getting close to another human being. Greg was terribly frightened of letting anybody in. His entire adult life was centered around protecting his inner feelings from intrusion. Therapy meant breaking down the walls he had spent a lifetime building. The idea frightened him.

He didn't show up for his fourth appointment. When I called him, he said therapy wasn't helping him and he didn't want to return. I never saw or heard from him again.

Accepting the patient's decision to quit therapy prematurely is never easy, just necessary. People like Greg, who walk a tightrope of normalcy, are constantly in fear of falling. The intimacy that therapy demands creates a feeling of plummeting into an abyss of unknown and dreaded emotions. Many are simply not ready for the challenge.

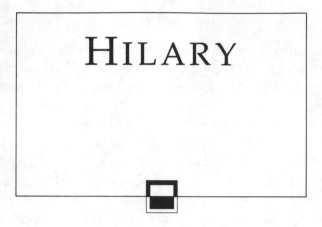

HILARY

APHRODITE'S ADDICTION

Meeting Hilary for the first time presented a problem. I didn't know where to rest my eyes. Her beauty was so complete, every feature competed for my attention. Her straight auburn hair touched her waist and reflected light in a way that dazzled me. Her flawless skin made me feel as if I were looking at a painting rather than a real person. Then there was her body—certainly *it* must have been Vargas's original inspiration.

Only by staying connected to her eyes did I notice any imperfection. Deep down inside her large brown eyes was a revealing sadness. Momentarily stunned by her beauty, I forgot she was human and wondered what a goddess like this could find so sad.

In fact, Hilary's life was in shambles. When she made the initial appointment to see me, she requested two hours. One hour would only scratch the surface, she said. It's unusual for patients to make a request for more than the normal hour session. I'm intrigued by the few who do because, quite frequently, they have a flair for the dramatic. As it turned out, Hilary was no exception. (Her beauty, of course, was certainly dramatic, but there was a great deal more about Hilary that was theatrical.) Dressed casually but impeccably, Hilary seated herself down in one of my barrel chairs, kicked off her shoes, tucked her feet up under her, flipped her long hair behind her with a whipping motion, and talked nonstop for an hour and a half.

The majority of my patients are hesitant upon first meeting me, asking me for direction on where to begin. What do I think is important, what do I want to know? Hilary, on the other hand, didn't miss a beat. She seemed to know exactly what she wanted me to know. Breathlessly, she began our first session talking about her current lover. It's not equally easy to listen to patients tell their stories, but Hilary was a good storyteller, using her hands and eyes to emphasize the points she wanted to make and rarely pausing to gather her thoughts. Later, when I found out she made her living as an actress, I experienced one of those "of course" feelings. If it hadn't been for her constant habit of fiddling with her hair, she would have given a perfect performance.

It felt like a performance because Hilary seemed so detached from her words, as if she was telling me about a good friend or a character in a script rather than herself. This style she had of distancing herself from her emotions caused me to take note. When I see this style of relating, I become sensitive to the person's issues of control, the need to appear self-contained and in charge of his or her emotions. I wondered how much of it was an act. Hilary, so intent on creating a certain impression, didn't notice that her emotions were not quite matching her words. Instead, her concentration was focused on telling me about Sam. The last two years of her life had been consumed by Sam. According to Hilary, her life had become Sam. "Nothing else seems to matter", she said. While she talked about being obsessed by him, I couldn't help but notice the paradox: She talked in such a controlled fashion about being out of control.

In his mid-thirties, Sam was sexy, successful, and solicitous, the Prince Charming who cast a magic spell over her. The first few months of their relationship had been marvelous. She had never been so happy. They went away for three-day weekends; they went to athletic events, to fancy restaurants, to the racetrack; and they went shopping—a lot. Sam liked to buy things for Hilary, expensive things that adorned her body. For Hilary, it was a fairy tale come true.

It wasn't that Hilary wasn't accustomed to attention from men. In fact, Hilary, at twenty-eight, had received more attention than most women get in a lifetime. "When I walk into a room, people stare," she said, not in an arrogant way, but rather matter-of-factly. Again, I felt a certain discrepancy here between her words and the emotional content. It was obvious that Hilary was intense, driven by her need to talk about Sam, as if talking about him to someone else would confirm her reality. This is something we all do at times. We talk to others about what disturbs us in an attempt to get confirmation for how we see things. We're not searching for enlightenment or knowledge at these times. Consequently, when we get contradictory rather than confirming feedback, we feel very misunderstood. Right now, Hilary needed a good listener, nothing else.

She wanted me to know Sam was different from the other men in her life. She didn't know why he was so different— just that he commandeered her life like no other man had. Within a month after they started dating, there was talk about love and exclusivity. With these magical words, Hilary began dreaming of marriage, family, and a future with Sam. Sam made promises, Hilary believed them. Why not? Didn't he show his love in every way possible? Hilary thought she had finally found what had been eluding her for years—a relationship built on love, a powerful attraction, and trust. That is, until she found out about Melanie.

The tip had come, "believe it or not," from an anonymous caller—a woman who simply said, "You don't really believe he loves only you, do you?" and then hung up. The call not only scared Hilary but filled her mind with disturbing questions. Who could this person be? Why would she want to do this? How did she get her number? And most scary of all, was it true? Was there somebody else?

She knew she had to talk to Sam about it, but she put it off for days. At first she didn't know exactly why she was so hesitant to tell him. Finally, after days of soul-searching, she realized she was avoiding discussing it with him because she was afraid it might be true. In a moment of clarity, she admitted to herself that she didn't know if she could believe what he would say. This thought scared her even more. Until the call, she had no reason to believe Sam was anything but truthful with her. So where was the doubt coming from? Why the hesitation to talk to him? She knew the smart thing to do was to give him the benefit of the doubt rather than assume he was guilty of cheating on her.

She was mustering the courage to talk to him when suddenly discussing it became moot. A week after the anonymous call, and on the evening she planned to bring it up, Sam broke a date with her. Hilary remained composed on the phone, even sounding understanding about his excuse. Inside she was seething.

After she hung up, her anger caused her to search back through the last months. As she did, she realized that this had happened before. He had broken several dates with her, making excuses about business meetings with some vague explanations about people arriving unexpectedly from out of town. Then a very strange sensation hit her—a déjà vu-like experience. She couldn't get a picture of where or when she'd been in this place before, but somehow she knew she'd been there a long time ago. She felt shaky inside and knew she had to lie down. Despair and depression followed, and a tremendous sadness wrapped itself around her like a wet blanket. She knew she was going to cry, but suddenly, she was overwhelmed instead by lethargy. She couldn't cry because she was too tired. Maybe she'd just go to sleep and never wake up.

As she was on the verge of falling asleep, an idea came to her. It was impulsive, childish, even dangerous, but she would risk it. She would follow him. Once she thought of it, it no longer felt like a choice to her. She felt compelled to know the truth, and, instinctively, she knew somehow that she wouldn't get that from Sam. The tiredness left her and was replaced by a surge of adrenaline, causing her heart and her mind to race. Exactly how would she pull it off? Once she started thinking about it, it didn't seem all that difficult.

She made a few calls to friends, making up a story about her car being out of commission. Finally, she found some-one who would lend her a car. Now she needed a disguise. She pulled out a wide-brimmed hat from the back of her closet. With a different car and a hat to cover her distin-guishing hair, Hilary thought she could get away without being recognized. She took a taxi to her friend's house and picked up the car. She drove around the corner, out of sight from her friend's, pulled her hair back in a ponytail, and stuffed it up under the hat. Then she drove to Sam's house, waiting outside for him to leave.

Not wanting to take a chance on missing him, she had arrived late in the afternoon. It was barely light outside, and, luckily for Hilary, his car was still parked in the drive-way. She parked a few houses away and slid down in the seat. Then she realized she might have to wait for some time. She hadn't given much thought to what it would be like for her to wait. It was going to be tough. She felt stupid, and her stomach was tied up in terrible knots. Inside her head, the doubts were like a three-ring circus. I'm behaving desperately, she thought. Just go home, forget about your suspicions, talk to Sam. Instead, she waited, transfixed by some deep need to know what Sam would really do.

To Hilary it seemed like hours before Sam finally left.

Actually, she had been there just under an hour, but her uncertainty about what she was doing clouded her ability to judge the time. Following him was easier than she had anticipated. She had worried she would lose him in traffic, especially if he went on the freeway. But he didn't go that far. Within five minutes, he pulled up in front of a small apartment house, got out of the car, went to one of the upstairs apartments, opened the door with a key, and disappeared inside. Once again, the issue of waiting confronted her, causing her uncertainty to surface once more. Hilary had no idea how long she should wait. She had never gotten that far in her thinking. For the first time since she received the anonymous phone call, she laughed. I wouldn't make a very good detective, she thought. She waited a half hour or so before finally convincing herself that sitting in a borrowed car with a hat as a disguise was ridiculous. She wasn't brave enough to go inside the apartment, and if Sam came out, he might somehow discover her. Then what would she do? She wasn't ready to confront him. Besides, she wanted to know more about who, if anybody, lived in that apartment. She left, but not without making note of how to return to the apartment.

She didn't recognize it at the time, but knowing who Sam was with and what he was doing became an obsession. She could think of nothing else. Her behavior, she claimed, seemed robotlike, as if she was being programmed by some remote-control device to do what she was doing. With a sheepish grin she told me she actually "staked out" the apartment where Sam had gone.

She went so far as to rent a car and on subsequent days drove over to the apartment, parking outside for an hour or two, hoping to see someone coming or going. She didn't know what or whom she expected to find, but she did it anyway. So, when she finally did see a woman leaving the apartment, she was caught off guard. It wasn't until she saw a real person that she realized she did have expectations. The woman Hilary saw leaving the apartment was ordinary, even somewhat dumpy. A woman, in Hilary's estimation, close to forty, twelve years her senior. At first she was relieved. This wasn't a woman with whom Sam could be romantically involved. She wasn't his type.

There must be some other explanation. Perhaps it was his sister. But why would Sam want to keep her from knowing he had a sister? And why did he lie to her about where he was going that night? Then an even more devastating thought crossed her mind. Maybe he was having an affair with her. That would mean this ordinary woman was attractive to him, that Hilary wasn't enough for him and that he needed more than she could give. A cold shiver ran through her body as these last possibilities crossed her mind. It was followed by a sickening feeling deep within her. Driving back to her apartment, Hilary felt as if she might throw up. Several times she had to pull the car over and take some deep breaths. Once inside her apartment, she could no longer control the sickening feeling. She threw up until nothing but dry heaves remained. Then she fell into the bed, physically and mentally exhausted. Even the exhaustion, however, didn't put a stop to her tortured suspicions.

She didn't sleep that night or for many nights afterward. The weariness she had first experienced after Sam broke the date persisted. It was a weariness unrelieved by sleep, which now seemed precious to her. Sometimes, by three or four in the morning, she would drift into a restless sleep, only to wake up several hours later with recurrent fantasies of Sam with this ordinary woman. A panicky feeling always followed and along with it the same question: Was he having sex with her? This thought made her nauseated each time it crept into her mind. She fought with it, but it seemed like a parasite determined to unleash its destruction on her.

A week went by, then another, and still she said nothing about her discovery to Sam. Promises to herself that she would always ended with her silence. Why couldn't she just talk to him? She was driving herself crazy with these suspicions while at the same time trying to act "normal" when with him. He never said anything to her about her behaving strangely. Her apparently brilliant acting skills were little consolation for the pain she was feeling.

Sex challenged her talent most. What used to be heaven now became an elaborate contrivance. She faked her own arousal and found that she was surprisingly good at it. To help the pretense along, she developed a fantasy. At first, the fantasy was a simple distraction, designed to facilitate her ruse. In her fantasy, Hilary would tease Sam with her sexual powers until he reached a peak arousal. Then, when he could stand it no more, she would walk away. He would be reduced to pleading with her to return. The most important part of the fantasy was the hurt on his face as she walked out on him, and it was this image that provided Hilary with sexual pleasure and eventual climax.

Without really knowing it was happening, the charade took on a life of its own. Hilary turned her suspicions into an elaborate game. The better she got at it, the less pain she felt, and the fantasy of wanting to hurt him receded into some dark place, a place Hilary didn't want to explore. Instead, she turned up the charm as easily as you would a gas flame. And she began to make demands, only Sam didn't recognize them as demands, disguised as they were by Hilary's superb seduction skills. Their evenings out now required that Sam spend even more money. The restaurants became fancier, the weekends away more luxurious, and the shopping trips more frequent. Hilary found that with the right look, lick of the lips, or a subtle placement of a hand on Sam's thigh, she could get him to buy her whatever she wanted.

The anonymous caller and the ordinary woman began to fade from Hilary's thoughts along with her suspicions. The night she had followed Sam seemed more like a dream than a reality. She started sleeping better and even considered trying to go on some auditions. Then, as if reality decided to slap her in the face, Sam broke another date with her.

As soon as he made his excuse on the phone, she knew she would follow him again.

She repeated her previous plan, borrowing a car, donning the brimmed hat, and following Sam as he left his house. Again, he went straight to the same apartment. Hilary didn't wait around this time. She left, drove home, took some sleeping pills, and cried herself to sleep, promising herself she would confront Sam this time. She had to know what Sam was doing in that apartment.

The next day her resolve held strong and she kept her promise. Sam picked her up for one of their many late-Sunday brunches. She decided it would be best to talk in public where she would be more likely to keep her composure. She would wait until they had eaten and were lingering over their coffee the way they always did. In the past this had been one of Hilary's favorite times. The Saturday-afternoon shopping, the evening's erotic adventure, and then the late-Sunday brunch. On Sundays they would look into each other's eyes and smile, communicating nonverbally the private secret of intimacy shared in the previous twenty-four hours.

This Sunday was different, of course. She didn't remember what she ordered, how the food tasted, or even if she ate anything. She only remembered feeling very panicky and wanting Sam to hurry up. It seemed like he was taking forever. Finally, the waitress cleared the plates, poured them more coffee, and left the bill. Hilary took a deep breath and began talking. Instead of her well-thought-out introduction, however, she found herself blurting it all out with a vengeance she didn't know she had.

"Who is the woman you visited last night?" she demanded to know.

"What are you talking about, Hilary? I was at a business meeting. I told you that."

"You're lying. How can you look straight at me and lie?"

"Why would I lie to you? I have nothing to lie about."

Hilary stared at Sam. He was so composed. So undaunted. "God! You're such a prick. I followed you last night and I know where you went. You were with a woman. Who is she?"

"You followed me? Why would you do that?" Even now Sam seemed so self-assured, so totally nondefensive.

"Because somebody called me and said you were cheating on me."

"Who called you?"

"Does it matter?"

"Yes, it matters to me." Very gently, as if concerned for Hilary rather than himself, Sam asked, "Who was it who called you?"

"I don't know," Hilary sighed. She could feel herself backing down, losing her resolve. Sam's calmness was so disconcerting. "It was a woman. She said, 'You don't think he loves only you, do you?' Then she hung up."

Sam didn't divert his eyes from Hilary's for even a second. Those eyes were now consuming hers, draining Hilary's courage. His stare told her nothing, so Hilary found herself saying things she never intended. "I thought I could get those words out of my head, but I can't . . . I thought I trusted you, but I don't . . . so, I followed you. Actually, I've followed you twice, after the last two dates you broke."

Hilary knew her words were sounding like a confession, not an accusation. Why was she on the defensive? It was Sam who was lying. Trying to regain her advantage she said more forcefully, "Both times you went to this woman's apartment. Who is she, Sam?" The panicky feeling left Hilary for a moment. Finally, she had told Sam what she knew and was actually relieved. The ball was in his court now.

Sam leaned forward on the table with his elbows, one hand went up to his mouth, and he kept running his fingers around the outside of his lips. It was the only sign he gave of being at all disturbed. He didn't answer at first and he didn't take his eyes away from hers.

As the seconds passed and Sam said nothing, Hilary

could feel the panicky feeling start to return. She felt a pain in her stomach, and she was sure everyone in the restaurant could hear her heart beat. What if Sam got angry at her for following him, she thought? He might go away. Then what? Part of her wanted to take back her words. But another part knew she had done the right thing. The part that knew she was doing the right thing was also telling her to shut up and let Sam feel the pressure of *her* silence. Just don't say a thing, she reminded herself again and again.

Finally, Sam removed his hand from his mouth and reached for hers. He brought her hand to his lips and kissed it sweetly. Not once taking his eyes from hers, he very calmly said, "She's nothing to me, Hilary. I promise I won't see her again."

It wasn't what Hilary expected. She had expected him to deny it. No, she had hoped he would deny it or at least convince her it never happened. In her mind she had invented a possible story: that the woman was an old housekeeper of his, that she was in the country illegally and Sam was secretly helping her. He didn't tell her any story. Instead, he was admitting that he was involved with her. She fought back the tears. When she had imagined this scene, she had remained strong. She was determined now that Sam would not see her cry. Instead, she'd give him a dose of his own medicine. Pulling her hand away from his, but continuing to keep the constant eye contact, she calmly said, "I can't trust you, Sam. You lied to me." And then she found herself saying what she promised a hundred times she wouldn't. "She isn't even pretty. What does she give you that I don't?"

"I told you, Hilary. She's nothing to me. She's just someone I knew before I met you. It's you I want." He paused at this point and once again took her hand. For the first time his eyes left hers and moved down to look at her hand. Under his breath he softly said, "I know I've hurt you. What can I do to make up for that?" Once again looking directly into her eyes, he asked, "How can I prove to you that I mean it when I say I'm through with her?"

Hilary found herself not needing to answer Sam's question. She just wanted things to be the way they used to be. In all her imagining of this conversation, she had never gotten this far. She had never allowed herself to believe that she would break it off or that Sam would no longer be in her life. Perhaps, now that she had confronted Sam, the whole mess would just go away. He *would* never see her again. They could go back to their wonderful weekends and she could go on with her life. She leaned forward and with the back of her hand she stroked Sam's cheek. "I love you and I really believe you love me. You must never see this woman again, Sam. I can't live like that."

"You won't regret this, Hilary. You and I were meant for each other. We both know that." He grabbed for the check, left a larger-then-necessary tip, and stood up. "Let's get out of here. I have something I want to show you. I know you'll like it, and on your body it's going to look too delicious to resist."

The long, romantic weekends resumed. So did the shopping. Hilary started sleeping again and her dreams of marrying Sam returned. Sam didn't break any more dates with her, and after six months his infidelity seemed like just a bad dream. Then, one Saturday afternoon when he told her he would be sailing, Hilary, returning from lunch with her mother, drove past a local restaurant and thought she saw Sam's car. She drove on, thinking her mind was playing tricks on her. Suddenly she knew she had to find out. She turned around and went back to the restaurant, pulling into the parking lot and driving up next to the car. She was right, it was his car. A nauseous feeling immediately came over her and she felt weak, but she knew she had to find out if he was with this woman.

She parked her car, entered the restaurant, and right away spotted Sam at a table. Across from him was the same ordinary woman. She felt shaky and enraged at the same time. Without even thinking what she would say or do, she walked over to the table. Sam looked up just as she was approaching. For the first time since she had known him, Hilary saw Sam lose his composure. As her hand picked up a glass of wine, her mind flashed to thoughts of scenes from a "B" movie. The next thing she knew she was dumping the wine all over him. Then she turned and left, without a word being spoken. Her head was pounding and she wasn't sure her legs would hold her up long enough to get out of the restaurant. So, when she finally did get outside, she thanked God for small favors. She wanted to go home before she embarrassed herself in the parking lot by throwing up.

As she was climbing back into her car, Sam came up behind her. He grabbed her by the shoulders and turned her around to face him. "Hilary, it's not what you think. Let me take you back to my place and we'll talk."

Hilary wanted to scratch his eyes out. Instead, she felt overwhelmed, defeated. She knew she couldn't drive in the state she was in. A feeble "all right" was all she could muster.

To make it worse, Sam didn't say a word in the car. He just looked straight ahead as if nothing had happened. Hilary was beside herself with emotions. She was angry and hurt, but more than that she was scared. The fear of losing Sam outweighed everything. Evidently, this woman must have some hold over Sam. She knew her jealousy was out of control, but she felt helpless to do anything different.

Once back at Sam's house, Hilary fell apart. She couldn't seem to stop crying. Sam tried to hold her, but she pushed him away. He sat, stoically and silently, across from her, waiting patiently for her to regain some control. Finally, when there were no tears left, Hilary asked him, "Why do you need this woman? Aren't I enough for you?'' Then she voiced her greatest fear: ''She must be giving you something sexually that I can't.''

''I don't know why I see her, Hilary. It's not the sex. No one has ever given me what you give me sexually. Anyway, it's not very often that I see her . . . maybe once every six weeks or so. Something comes over me and I feel the need to see her. Her name is Melanie and she's been in my life a long time, six years or more. I've never been in love with her. She accepts that and doesn't seem to care. She's known about you since we started dating, and she knows I love you.''

Hilary's mind was a mass of confusion. If Melanie wasn't important to Sam, why couldn't he stop seeing her? She simply didn't understand, but she knew she couldn't deal with Sam right now. Finally, she said, ''I can't see you for a while, Sam. I have to think this out. I don't want your promises anymore because I can't believe you. Take me back to my car and just leave me alone for a while. Don't call, don't come over. Just stay out of my life long enough for me to know what's best for me.''

Sam didn't try to argue with her. He drove her back to her car, followed her home to be sure she arrived safely, and, without walking her to the door, drove off.

But Sam didn't stay out of Hilary's life. He called constantly, pleading with her to see him, to talk to him. At first she hung up on him. Then she tried not answering the phone, but he would let it ring and ring. She tried unplugging it from the wall, but when he didn't get an answer, he would come over to her apartment, ring the bell, and bang on the door. Hilary would threaten to call the police if he didn't go away. The third time Sam did this, Hilary did call the police. Sam's belligerence resulted in their having to be forceful with him to get him to leave. Hilary watched all this with horror. She'd never seen Sam so angry.

Since the first anonymous phone call, Hilary had not slept well. Her nerves were raw. To make it worse, she felt terrible about having called the police. She started to worry that maybe she had overreacted, and the fear that Sam might actually go away for good returned. She realized that being without Sam just didn't seem like a choice to her. She finally called Sam and said she would have dinner with him—just to talk. Once again she heard him say, ''You won't regret this.''

Within a couple of hours after hanging up the phone, a dozen red roses were delivered to her home, followed shortly by another delivery, a beaded dress that Hilary felt sure must have cost more than a thousand dollars. Without trying it on, Hilary knew it would fit perfectly. He was trying to soften her, she thought. But she was determined not to let these material things influence her. She hadn't really decided to give Sam a second chance; she'd only agreed to have dinner so they could talk. But when he produced a diamond ring at dinner and asked her to marry him, her resolve quickly vanished.

This is what she had wanted: to be Sam's wife. Now he was giving her the chance. She knew she'd have to forgive him to get what she wanted. Last week, forgiving him had seemed impossible; tonight it seemed easy. She took the ring, thinking that marriage might just do away with Melanie forever. Once she had the ring on her finger, she could feel the shattered pieces of herself being pulled together again. But when Sam asked her to set a wedding date, she refused. Something deep inside her told her there would always be danger where Sam was involved. Still, living without Sam had been unmanageable. Being engaged would buy her some time to figure it all out.

Their life went back to the familiar routine. The three-day weekends were now more frequent, and the shopping expeditions grew to be a pattern. What also became a pattern was Hilary's driving by Melanie's apartment. When she wasn't with Sam for the day, Hilary would drive by, park the car, and wait. The amount of time she waited varied. On one occasion when she actually saw Melanie, she followed her. When Melanie ended up at the grocery store, Hilary felt foolish. Yet she didn't stop her tracking. She couldn't prove it, but intuitively, she knew Sam was still seeing Melanie. A compulsive need to know for sure finally resulted in her taking drastic action. She would set Sam up. She told him she was going out of town to see her sister. Instead, she once again staked out Melanie's place. Her intuition paid off.

When she saw Sam drive up, something inside of her gave way, and her whole body went limp. This time she didn't feel nauseated, she just felt drained. She knew she couldn't fight anymore. There was no point in confronting him because she couldn't live without him. Her threats were useless; she couldn't back them up. Apparently, Sam was as unable to live without Melanie as Hilary was without Sam. The whole messy thing was really sick. She knew she needed some help. That's when she called me.

As I listened to Hilary the day of our first meeting, I realized that she was obsessed by Sam. Without him, she felt incomplete, unable to cope in a world that looked dreary. Being with him gave her a high she couldn't get on her own. When she was with Sam, the world looked rosy. Yet, as with all obsessions, the dependency on the obsession was all-consuming, in the same way that an addict's addiction becomes all-consuming. The life of an addict becomes a series of highs followed by lows, which create the obsessive search to regain the high. It's a circular trap without a beginning or an end. It takes on a life of its own with a force greater than the human being who's trapped in it.

When a person becomes obsessed by another person, regardless of how badly she may be treated, it's usually because the object of the obsession fills some emotional void in her life. She stays in the relationship because she can't give up the fantasy that the other person will fill this emotional void. At this point in Hilary's treatment, I wasn't yet sure of what Sam represented to her. But I've seen this blind devotion before in men and women who are repeatedly abused by their mates yet stubbornly cling to the false belief that next time it will be different.

Hilary had told me a great deal in an hour and a half, but there was much still to know and understand. We both needed to know what was creating the desperation, what void she was trying to fill. Because I believe in a school of thought known as *developmental psychology*, I knew her past held the answers to this question. As we grow, life is continually presenting opportunities for us to develop either healthy or unhealthy coping behaviors. What we eventually become as adults is dependent upon a mixture of biology and our particular life experiences. During childhood, the personality is very vulnerable because it's still in the molding stage. Unfortunately, life sometimes overwhelms the developing personality and sets the stage for future problems.

I think of the personality or ego as being constructed much like a house or other building. It needs a strong foundation and many supporting structures to weather the storms of life. The people in our lives act as the construction workers, life experiences as the materials for our building. Careless workers or faulty materials can easily create a weak link in the structure. Once built in and covered by an external shell, the weakness remains, perhaps unnoticed, until life stresses challenge the fragile point. Correcting the weakness may mean removing the outer shell and tearing down much of the structure to find the weak link. That's what was in store for Hilary and me. Until we found the weak link, we couldn't repair or fortify the ego, and Hilary would be destined to repeat the pattern.

At the end of her story, Hilary gave a very forlorn sigh and said, "I know I should leave him. He can't be trusted. Yet, I go on trying to make this relationship work. What is it about him that makes me feel so helpless?"

It was natural for Hilary to be looking outward to find the weak link because we all develop defenses to cover up our vulnerabilities. Often, the defenses are so successful that we stop knowing who we really are. At this point, we blame others for our vulnerability. Perhaps the best-known example is the dynamic of the rescuer/victim. A rescuer's weak link is his desperate need to be needed. In order to meet that need, he "falls" for a person whose weak link is the need to feel victimized. In his desperation, he fails to see his own need but chooses to focus on the other person's weakness.

A therapist has to be careful not to fall prey to a patient's need to blame others for his or her own vulnerabilities. It was easy in this situation to make Sam the bad guy. After all, he was the one who cheated and lied. Much of the dramatics of Hilary's story was aimed at convincing me what a louse Sam really was. I had to be careful. Colluding with Hilary on this would be dangerous because blaming Sam would only serve to get Hilary off the hook. Besides, in any relationship dynamic, it takes two individuals, each feeding the other's vulnerabilities, for it to continue.

At the moment, all I could work with was Hilary's perspective. With couples, I usually encourage the partner to come in at least for a few sessions to present his or her point of view. Otherwise, I'm dealing with "secondhand" information. So, I asked Hilary if she thought Sam would be willing to see me. She was emphatic about not having him involved.

"He'll somehow manage to talk me out of this if he knows about it. I don't want to tell him. It will make him angry and I'm afraid of his anger, so I do anything he says. I feel helpless when it comes to Sam."

"When you talk about your helplessness, I get a mental image of a force much greater than you. A picture of a giant magnet comes to mind. The magnet is sucking you toward it and you don't have the strength to fight it," I said.

"Yes. Exactly. It feels really powerful. Like I'm helpless to break the connection. God! I hate feeling out of control."

"Do you often feel out of control?"

"No. As long as I can remember, I've felt I had the upper hand. But Sam is different. That's why I knew I needed help. Can you help me?"

"Help you with what?"

Hilary shifted in her chair, once again flipped the few loose strands of long hair behind her, and didn't speak for a moment. When she finally did, she said, "Good question. I guess I don't know what I want. I know the right answer would be that I need help in getting Sam out of my life. But I'm not ready for Sam to be out of my life."

"What do you think you are ready for?"

"When I called you, I thought I was ready to learn more about me—about why Sam has so much control over me and about why I . . ." Hilary stopped in midsentence and said instead, "Now that I'm here, I'm not so sure I want to know about me. There's stuff I haven't told you, weird stuff I haven't told anybody." These last words were almost mumbled, and for the first time in the almost two hours of being with Hilary, I saw a slight loss of composure and of playing a role.

I knew now that we were dealing with something very familiar to a sex therapist: secrets. Sexual secrets, the producers of guilt and shame, the genesis of moral turpitude, the agents of depravity. To those who hold them, the world seems a very unforgiving place. I knew now that Hilary was being controlled by a deep sense of shame and that it might be some time before I found out exactly what was causing her to reproach herself.

"When it feels right, you'll tell me," I replied.

There was a noticeable sigh of relief before Hilary asked, "Meantime, what do I do about Sam? He keeps pressuring me to set a wedding date."

"From what you've told me so far, I have a strong feeling that he'll wait. What do you think?"

A slight smile crossed her face and then she said, "Yes, I think you're right. He'll wait."

As it turned out, it didn't take all that long for Hilary to reveal the "weird" stuff. Little by little in the next several sessions she began to talk about her secret. It centered around the shopping trips and what they came to mean to her. The trips had begun "innocently." Sam had told her that she was the most beautiful woman he had ever seen and that he enjoyed taking her out and showing her off by having her try on beautiful clothes. She knew he was proud to be with her, and she loved the feeling this gave her. There was a vague feeling of discomfort about exhibiting herself in the way Sam liked, but the discomfort was always overpowered by the exhilarating feeling of being "shown off." The discomfort soon disappeared altogether.

After she found out about Melanie, she noticed that she began to daydream during the week about the shopping trips. In her daydreams, it was lingerie, not clothes, that she was trying on for Sam. In real life, she found it didn't take much persuasion to get Sam into the lingerie department. And she had to admit she liked to try on the lingerie, parading each of the items in front of Sam and making him select what he liked best. She turned it into an elaborate foreplay experience, and by the time the shopping trip was over, Sam would be beside himself. If they were in town, Hilary would insist they go to a hotel rather than back to Sam's house. She said it would be more exciting that way, but somehow she knew it was more than just that. It *had* to be a hotel. Otherwise, it wasn't right. She couldn't explain this to herself, she just knew it had to be. Once in the hotel room, they would order champagne and food from room service, and then the game would begin.

During these rendezvous, Hilary felt a devilish side of her she had not experience before. Trying on the lingerie and feeling its texture against her skin brought out a new personality. This part of her personality, the sexual part, felt driven, as if out of her control. She was scared by this unfamiliar side of herself. But there was an excitement to the whole experience that thrilled her as well. It was the exhilaration that seemed to take charge and caused all inhibitions to melt away. She loved teasing Sam into a frenzy before allowing intercourse to occur. Then she would slip into her fantasy of abandoning him while he pleaded with her not to leave. Only in this way could she receive any sexual pleasure for herself.

The weeks went by and the shopping sprees continued. Hilary's closet began to look like a lingerie shop. She never took the tags off the items Sam bought. It was the one thing she insisted on; the tags were not to be removed. She liked to stand back and look at all the beautiful, lacy items. Then she would touch them with her hands and rub them lightly against her face and her body. Once her body was in contact with the silky texture of the material, a warm, secure feeling would flow through her, causing an intense sexual arousal, relieved only by masturbation, and only if accompanied by the fantasy of Sam's pleading with her not to leave.

It was somewhere around the sixth or seventh session that Hilary finally completed her "confession," as she called it. "That's it," she said. "There isn't any more to tell. Have you ever heard such a perverted story?" she asked rather flippantly.

"What do you mean by perverted?" I asked.

Hilary flashed angry eyes at me and said, "You know damn well that collecting lingerie to masturbate to is pretty kinky stuff.'' Then she started to cry. At first she fought the tears, but when she picked up the tissue box it signaled something in her. The dam broke and she gave in; the tears turned into deep sobs. She kept pulling tissues from the box. First she tried dabbing at her mascara, but when the tears kept coming she finally just wiped her eyes, using tissue after tissue. I couldn't help noticing how neatly she laid the used tissues in a pile on her lap. After about five minutes, she began to regain some control. She straightened up in the chair, once again whipped her long hair behind her, and asked, ''Do I have black stuff all over my face?''

I wasn't surprised when Hilary didn't show up for her next appointment. It's not unusual for the initial good feelings of relief from sharing a carefully guarded secret to fade, leaving humiliation in their place. Facing the humiliation would be especially difficult for Hilary, who prided herself on being in control. In admitting her secret to me, Hilary had, at the same time, stopped hiding from herself. Now exposed, she was really scared—she wasn't so sure she wanted to know this shameful part of her. Having someone else know about it was even more difficult. These feelings were most likely causing her to play several elaborate, unconscious mind games.

First, if she didn't have to face me, maybe she could go back to denying the existence of the embarrassing behavior. Because she had told me, I would always be an anchor to the reality of the behavior, a sort of proof of its existence. If she could get me out of the picture, she could stop being reminded.

Secondly, but more importantly, she would leave me before I could leave her. Sexual secrets exist because we fear rejection upon discovery of what we interpret as shameful behavior. In her mind, she was sure I could feel only disgust toward her now that I knew her secret. My disgust must surely lead to abandonment.

These two fears, humiliation and abandonment, will eventually emerge in any therapy situation in which tightly guarded shameful secrets are disclosed. The disclosure acts as the turning point in the therapy. Confronting the fears means progress, while running away from them means stagnation. Hilary would not conquer her addiction to Sam or to the lingerie until she faced these fears and gave herself the opportunity to stop being afraid. Therapy, because it means confronting fears, almost always presents an ambivalent situation.

Pushing past the ambivalence is essential to overcoming the fear. I feel strongly that patients have to do this on their own. Only rarely will I call a patient who has missed a session, and never do I try to convince a patient to return to therapy. Internal motivation is the key to successful therapy, not pleasing or appeasing the therapist.

So, when Hilary called me several days after the missed appointment, I knew she had made a personal decision. She was an emotional wreck, she said. She began explaining to me what had happened. Without pausing between thoughts, she quickly recounted the last week. She had made a last-minute decision to take a small part in a movie, which required her to go out of town on a three-day shoot. It had been months since she last worked, and Sam had been paying for everything. She had decided to take the small part just to get back into things slowly—she would need her work again if she were going to live without Sam. But once away from home, she had fallen apart. Her anxiety about performing interfered with her ability to keep her lines straight. She had quit after an embarrassing scene with the director and had taken the next plane home. Then, a pause, followed by three successive questions. Why was she destroying the one thing that brought her success? Was she really that self-destructive? Could I see her right away?

Even though Hilary didn't know she was doing it, I knew

I was being put to the ultimate test. Would I "take her back" after she had told me about her shameful secret and on top of that stood me up? How much bad behavior would I tolerate before I rejected her? I could hear the surprise in her voice when I said I could see her the next day.

From the desperate way she had sounded on the phone, I guess I expected it to show on her. Instead, she arrived in my office in typical "Hilary fashion." Everything—the hair, the makeup, the clothes—was in perfect order. Outwardly, she looked as if the world was her oyster. Inside, however, I felt that the grain of sand was not creating a pearl but rather a crack in the fragile foundation. I wasn't sure what she was using to hold the outside together because I knew that at any moment the inside could crumble.

She started the session with an apology. "I'm sorry about missing the appointment. I should have called you to tell you about taking the part in the movie."

"Why didn't you?"

"I got busy with making plans to leave, and I guess I forgot."

"Perhaps you just didn't want to face me after telling me such private things."

"Well, I guess that was part of it. I was embarrassed." She looked away for a moment and then back at me. "But I'm back now. I don't know if I'm ready to face what I'm hiding, but I don't think I have a choice. This last week I've been totally self-destructive. It's possible I might have ruined my career for good. If I don't do something, I'm doomed. So, where do we start?"

"Well, I know your biggest concern is your present situation—what to do about Sam. But until we know more about your past, we can't understand your present behavior. Start by telling me about your family and your childhood."

Over the next few weeks I learned a great deal about Hilary, especially about her need for control. Her parents were blue-ribbon role models of control. During her early years and until she was ten years old, Hilary's mother had been a state congresswoman. When she left office, she remained extremely active in political affairs. Her father was a well-known and extremely successful attorney. Impressions and appearance were everything to both her parents. Hilary could remember only a few rare moments when they weren't on stage for someone else—or each other. Hilary had a sense that they competed with each other to see who could be the busiest, most sought-after person. Her mother was out of town a great deal, either at the state capital or at other pressing engagements around the country, sometimes the world. While her father didn't travel, he was seldom at home. At first, Hilary looked forward to those special times when he would walk in the door and she was still awake. Soon, however, she came to realize that "important" telephone calls would keep him from spending time with her.

An only child, Hilary felt she must have been an accident. How could people so busy really want a child? she often wondered. She had lots of time to think about such things. With no siblings and no playmates (arranging playmates took parental time), Hilary spent a great deal of her early years alone or with her nanny. Hilary couldn't remember too much about her nanny, but she did remember that when she was about four years old, the nanny went away for a few months. She didn't know why she left, only that she was glad she was gone. Only then did she spend more time with her parents, especially her father. These short few months were a very happy time for Hilary, even though she recalled her parents being very upset about it disrupting their schedules. Eventually, the nanny returned and the special times with her father stopped. With the return of her nanny came the return of Hilary's loneliness.

Hilary didn't remember many specifics about her preschool years. It did sink in at a very young age, however, that her parents were very important people, somehow special. They were always being invited places by other important people. The unmemorable nanny imparted one memorable message: Be a good girl and don't cause problems for these important people.

Quiet, compliant, and pleasing, Hilary obviously learned the lesson well. Her "good" behavior resulted in her being mostly ignored. But there were certain occasions on which she received lots of attention from lots of people. She had vivid memories of being dressed by her nanny to make an "appearance" at one or another of the many parties that were held at her large home. At first she felt uncomfortable being the center of attention; eventually, however, she grew to like the compliments and the great hoopla that she aroused when she entered a room. When she was younger, the words "precious," "adorable," and "darling" were used frequently. As she grew older the words changed: "beautiful," "charming," "stunning," "lovely"—these were words that Hilary grew to associate with her physical appearance. When Hilary walked into a room, she knew she made her parents proud. If only for a moment, Hilary's beauty allowed her to become their shining star.

Intuitively, Hilary came to understand that her beauty was a talisman. Both parents were continually reminding her "not to worry her pretty little head about it" whenever there was a problem. They would take care of it (or hire someone else to take care of whatever it was). Indirectly, Hilary had learned that appearance, not brains, was what counted. Not surprisingly, school presented some problems for Hilary, especially the academic classes. Making good grades didn't seem important to Hilary—or to her parents, for that matter. Occasionally, they would tell her she wasn't trying hard enough, but mostly they let her mediocre grades go unnoticed.

In the ninth grade, she traveled to New York with her father. Over the years, she had often traveled with him when he went East to visit his family. Even though Hilary received the same kind of reaction from his family that she received from his friends, she didn't like these trips, in which she had her father's undivided attention. At one time in her life, she would have been thrilled at the prospect of having him to herself. Somewhere along the way, this had changed. She didn't know why she felt this way. Her father seemed the same person he had always been—a real charmer.

However, this trip was different. It served as a turning point in her life. This time, she and her father went to see several plays, and from that moment on, Hilary knew what she would be when she grew up: a famous actress. Convinced that she had discovered her destiny, in the tenth grade she enrolled in a drama class. She was right; she loved acting. On the stage she felt alive, important, and successful. And it pleased her parents greatly. They agreed to outside acting classes, then hired acting coaches for her when she got the lead in the senior play. She was sensational and for days afterward received accolades from her friends. Her parents, who had taken time out from their busy schedules to attend the play, were quite impressed with their princess. This experience only reinforced Hilary's dream of becoming a famous actress.

Hilary didn't have as much success with boys. She knew she was the center of their attention when she walked into any room, but she didn't get called for dates. Her girlfriends told her the boys were afraid of her. She was *too* beautiful, they said. Hilary quickly lost interest in boys—their immaturity bored her. Instead, at seventeen, she turned her attention toward men. In this arena, she was extremely successful and very much in control, able to choose among many suitors, always several years her senior. She dated many but would allow few to occupy her time totally. She didn't want a steady beau who might get in the way of her acting career. Her parents didn't like her dating older men, but, as was their style, they voiced their objections weakly and in the end, let their many obligations take priority over their concerns for their daughter.

After Hilary graduated from high school, her mother pulled a few strings to get her into a college with a good reputation in drama. It was the first time having "important" parents worked in Hilary's favor. Academic work continued to be a struggle for Hilary, but the successes in acting kept her going. By the end of her four years, she had several agents interested in signing her. Although not a word was said, Hilary knew this time that it was her father who was using his influence. She didn't care. Everyone told her she was a good actress, but so were hundreds of others. In this business, knowing the right people was simply how the game was played. If she had a few "ins," so be it. It was the second time in her life she realized that having important parents could be an advantage rather than a disadvantage.

The years after college were good years for Hilary. Considering the difficulties of the career she chose, she was making steady progress. A two-year contract for a small part in a daytime soap had yielded enough money to pay the bills for a while. She had much higher aspirations than soaps, but the money was great, and now she could take her time while she searched for the right part in a movie.

Her social life was also running smoothly. Spending time alone was easy for her—after all, she had spent a great deal of her childhood with herself as company. Intentionally, she had only a few select female friends, but these were valued friendships that meant a great deal to her. She had no use for shallow friendships. Her parents' life had turned her off to that. And men? Well, they were hers for the asking. Strangely, though, she felt little need to date just to be dating. She knew marriage was something she wanted for the future, but she certainly didn't feel desperate. She could take her time and wait for the right man. All in all, Hilary had her life under control. That is, until she met Sam and it started to crumble around her. Now her life was a living nightmare over which she seemed to have no control. Again and again Hilary would ask herself why she was allowing this man to totally disrupt her carefully planned life. None of it made sense to her.

In the weeks that Hilary and I spent talking about her childhood years, I never once felt her attach an emotion to her history. She talked matter-of-factly about her parents' busy schedule, even, at times, defending their decision to leave their only daughter's life to others. She had perfected this outward shell of hers, which I suspected effectively kept the hurt of their rejection from penetrating her essence. I believed that, at a level intended to defend against the hurt, she had convinced herself that their importance warranted their lack of interest in their child. It made sense, then, that Hilary would not associate her childhood experiences with her current problems. In her mind, her parents' behavior was justified. Giving it justification allowed Hilary to disconnect from the pain. It just didn't occur to her that something in her past relationship with her parents could be causing her reaction to Sam.

But our past is always more important to our present than we realize. We spend a lot of our present life trying to resolve hurtful issues of our childhood. As in Hilary's case and many others, the determination to "get it right this time" becomes obsessive. There was a relationship between Hilary's parents' neglect and her current problems; we just hadn't discovered the specifics.

One thing was certain, however: It had something to do with sex. Some part of her sexuality was being threatened in the relationship with Sam. Never once in her recounting of her childhood did she mention any sexual memories, good or bad. She never remembered her parents' talking to her about the subject, and she had no memory of them ever being intimate with each other. Since she was an only child, she had never participated in the normal sexual exploration of siblings. Nor had she done this with any playmates. The only sexual memory of any significance she had dated back to high school, when she began dating older men. Hilary couldn't say how she knew, but she did know that sex would be expected. On her own, she had gotten birth-control pills. She wouldn't let a stupid mistake ruin the possibility of an acting career. She was sexual with most of the men she dated. Sex meant very little to her, but she was a good actress and knew how to please a man. Once out of college and invested in her career, she felt little need to "perform" sexually for men. Once again, however, Sam had turned Hilary's life upside down. She was now faced with a disturbing side of her sexual self she didn't know existed.

Most sexual obsessions are misguided attempts at rescuing some part of the sexual person. Exactly why Hilary had picked Sam, and why the lingerie, were not yet clear to me, but I knew Hilary had the answers buried in her memories. Our task was to dig deep enough to unearth the memories. Something in her past would eventually reveal the connection. Only then would it be possible to break that connection.

I suspected that her parents' indifference to Hilary was an important piece in this mysterious puzzle. Another significant piece of the puzzle had to be the attention she received as a result of her physical beauty. Even though Hilary dismissed both of these as irrelevant, I was unwilling to disregard their contribution. Before I could find exactly where they fit into the puzzle, however, I first had to fill in some other pieces.

I reviewed my notes of the sessions in which Hilary talked about her childhood, looking for the missing pieces. Like a detective, I searched for the "holes" in her story. What the patient doesn't tell you is as important as what she does tell you. The "cover-up" is just that—an attempt to keep something very painful out of conscious awareness. Hilary's mind was blocking, preferring instead to avoid the pain of the memory.

As I read and reread my notes, I was drawn again and again to the time in Hilary's life when her nanny left. This was a happy time for her. She recalled spending special time with her father. Later, she remarked that spending time with her father was uncomfortable. I couldn't help but wonder what caused this change. I made a note to explore this further with Hilary.

In the next session, I asked Hilary about the special times she spent with her father. "What can you tell me about those times? Can you remember what made them special?" I asked.

"Mostly, I remember just the good feelings. You know, something I looked forward to. The specifics are really vague. Except, I do remember getting dressed up to go out with him. He would help me pick out my dress." She stopped talking at this point and gazed into space for a few moments. Then, with moisture in her eyes, she reached for a tissue and said, "He called me his little princess."

"Why the tears, Hilary? What are you feeling?"

"I'm not sure. It feels mixed . . . fond memories with some great sadness. . . . It was so rare for him to spend Saturdays with me."

"You remember it being more than one Saturday?"

She paused before she answered. "Strange, I don't know why I said Saturday. It wasn't until just now that I realized it always was a Saturday. I know it was more than one but I can't tell you how many. Is it important?"

"Maybe. Do you remember why you got so dressed up? Were you going somewhere?"

"I can't remember exactly. I do remember driving in his car. I loved his car. It was long and black with lots of fancy dials inside. I'd sit in the front seat with him and sneak looks at him while he was driving. He was so handsome to me. I can remember feeling so proud to be with him."

"That feeling of loving to be with him eventually went away. Isn't that what you told me?"

"Yes. I don't know why. Later, when we would travel back East to visit his family . . . that was the only other time just the two of us would be together . . . I remember not wanting to look at him at all. In fact, I dreaded those trips. That is, until that time we went to the theater. That changed my life.

"You dreaded the trips?"

"Yes. Being around my father made me very uncomfortable." Suddenly, she shifted in her chair and reached for her hair, twisting it around and around her fingers. By now I recognized this behavior as a sign of her anxiety. We were getting close to something important but surely painful for Hilary. Then, rather abruptly, she asked, "Is any of this relevant to what's going on with me now?"

"I think so, Hilary. Your memory is blocked for a reason. Usually that reason is because what you're blocking out is pretty painful. I think it has to do with some unfinished business you have with your father."

"What makes you think it has something to do with my father?"

"Well, you remember treasuring the times you spent with him while your nanny was gone. The next memories you have, you're uncomfortable with him. Something must have happened to change those feelings."

"I've thought about this so many times over the years . . . wondering why I felt so uncomfortable with him. I've racked my brains and still, I just can't remember anything that would cause me to change the way I felt."

"Well, if what you're blocking is painful, you wouldn't easily remember."

"Is it really necessary that I remember?"

"Yes, it is. I think you experienced something—perhaps on those Saturdays—that you misinterpreted."

"Why do you think it happened on those Saturdays?"

"Because, even though they were special, you can't remember exactly how you spent them. And it seems that they were a turning point in your feelings toward your dad."

"What's that got to do with Sam? And with the lingerie?"

"They're connected, Hilary. But we won't know exactly how until we know what happened."

"Is there a way I can remember those Saturdays?"

"There are a few things we could try that would help you remember. But the memories won't be pleasant for you."

"So, what you're saying is I won't stop being destructive if I don't remember, but remembering will hurt?"

"Yes."

"That's pretty scary."

"Exactly. That's why you've blocked it all out."

"I still don't understand why remembering will help me to stop all this destructive behavior."

"Something very unpleasant happened to you as a child. What's happening to you now is an attempt to undo that earlier experience. Think of yourself as a playwright, obsessed with rewriting an earlier, disastrous script, so to speak and . . ."

"And," Hilary interrupted, "Sam is playing the part of my father."

"I believe he is."

"If that's true, I can't help but wonder if it's coincidence or by design that I'm an actress."

"It is curious, isn't it?"

"Carol, I'm just beginning to realize how curious life is. . . . Tell me more about these things we might do to help me remember."

Hilary and I were about to embark upon an experience in backward association. It's a technique often used in therapy to help a patient recall past blocked memories. It is done while the patient is in a relaxed, trancelike state. Current emotional content is taken back further and further in time in an attempt to bring into focus the original event. This is what transpired in our next session.

Hilary appeared in my office in jeans, an old sweatshirt, and sandals. But it wasn't only her clothing that stood out as uncharacteristic. There were two other noticeable differences in her appearance: She had no makeup on and her hair was tied back in a ponytail. In her hand she had a box of tissues. Even as "plain Jane" she still managed to be strikingly beautiful.

She held up the box of tissue and jokingly remarked, "I came prepared. I figured this would be a real tearjerker. No point in bothering with the makeup. By the time this is over, I'll be a mess, I'm sure."

"Obviously, you've been thinking about this."

"Haven't thought about much else since we talked last. I'm ready as I'll ever be. Can we get started? I want to stop thinking about it and just do it."

"Certainly. Why don't you get yourself in a very comfortable position and we'll begin."

Hilary settled down in the chair, letting her head rest on the back and stretching her long legs out in front of her. She placed both hands on the arms of the chair. "Ready?" I asked.

"Ready," she bravely answered.

"Close your eyes, Hilary, and just focus on the sound of my voice. I'm going to count from five down to one. With each count, I want you to take a deep breath and let your body relax further and further. Five . . . deep breath, let it out and relax, four . . . deep breath, double the relaxation . . . three, deep breath and relax, two . . . deep breath and relax, one . . . deep breath and relax. Now you are com-

73

pletely and totally relaxed. In this relaxed state you can concentrate more intensely than ever before.

"Right now I want you think back on a recent time in which you felt really lousy. Get a mental picture of yourself in that situation and tell me what the picture looks like."

"I'm seeing Sam sitting with Melanie in the restaurant." Hilary's words in no way reflected the pained look she had on her face as this image came to mind.

"Concentrate on this image, Hilary. Now tell me what you're feeling."

Again, a pained look crossed her face, and her hands tightly squeezed the arms of the chair. "I'm feeling sick," she answered. This time you could hear the shakiness in her voice.

"Describe the feeling to me, Hilary."

Her face contorted in a pained expression, marring her natural beauty. Almost choking on her words she barely managed to mumble, "I feel a pain in my chest. It hurts so much—like my heart is shattering in a million pieces. I feel weak, very weak, like I just want to lie down and go to sleep and never have to wake up again." Tears were running down the sides of her face, but Hilary didn't seem to notice.

"Have you had this feeling before, Hilary?"

"Yes."

"When?"

She didn't answer for a moment. I could see her eyes moving back and forth underneath her lids as if she were searching for a picture. Finally, she said, "Sam's going into Melanie's apartment . . . the night I followed him." The tears were turning into sobs. Hilary forgot all about the tissues she had so preparedly set in her lap, making attempts, instead, to wipe away the tears with her fists.

"Hilary, can you hear me?" I asked.

"Yes."

"Go back further in time. Did you ever have this feeling before you met Sam?"

"Yes."

"Tell me about it."

Again, I could see the movement of the eyes under the lids, as if she were scanning a screen searching for a particular part. The pained look on her face was still there, and her body was squirming in the chair. "I hear noises," she said.

"What kind of noises?"

"Sounds. I don't know what they are but I don't like them."

"Are you afraid?"

"Yes."

"Do you know what you're afraid of?"

"No."

"Do you know how old you are?"

"Little girl . . . afraid." Unexpectedly, Hilary opened her eyes and sat up in the chair. "I don't want to go on. Whatever it is, I don't want to remember it. It's too terrible. This isn't a good idea, and I don't think it's a good idea for me to come back. I'll get Sam out of my life without having to torture myself in this way." On that note, she picked up her purse and her tissue box and walked out of my office.

A month went by and I didn't hear from Hilary. I thought of her often, hoping she was somehow surviving her internal conflicts; surely they must be doing a frenetic war dance within her. I felt sure that the two opposing parts, each fighting for what it believed, were tearing her apart inside. One faction was fighting for freedom from her tortured past while another part, an apparently stronger rival, was fighting to keep the pain of the past from resurfacing.

One of the things a therapist has to accept is that he or she can't make the final decision for a patient. Some patients persevere and work through their pain while others feel too vulnerable to stay in the battle. Sometimes patients quit treatment in the middle. For a therapist, it's an impotent feeling to have a patient quit before a resolution. Because I believe so strongly that revealing is healing, I feel especially sad when I have a patient who feels a stronger need to avoid than confront painful memories.

So when I did receive a call from Hilary, I felt pleased that she was willing to try again to meet her fears head-on. She didn't make any excuses for her abrupt behavior in the last session. She simply asked if I would see her again. We set up an appointment for the following week.

When I saw her I was taken aback. She had lost a considerable amount of weight. Being one of God's few perfect creatures, on her it looked terrible. The color was gone from her face, and her skin had a drawn, pasty look. As if reading my mind, she began by saying, "I know what you're thinking. I look like shit. I've already been chastised by everyone I know, so don't even bother. I've been holed up in my apartment like a recluse. I can't sleep, and I guess I don't have to tell you I'm not eating. After I left our last session, I told Sam I didn't want to see him again. He told me I didn't really mean it." She gave a paltry laugh and said, "I told him to 'try me.' Well, that son of a bitch didn't call. It took only a couple of days for my resolve to vanish. Next thing I know I felt like I was going to die." Then, as if there was no fight left in her, she gave a big sigh and said, "I started with the lingerie again. I pulled it all out of my closet—every single piece of it—and piled it on my bed. I wrapped myself up in it and stayed that way for hours. It was the only way I could get any peace. I could sleep only if I masturbated with it surrounding me, covering me, almost smothering me.

"Finally, after about two weeks, I couldn't stand it any longer. I called him. He was cold . . . very angry, and he yelled at me. He said he was tired of my games, and if I wanted him back, I'd have to set a wedding date within six months. 'No more pissing around,' he said." She paused here and her eyes left mine and traveled around the room several times, finally coming back to meet mine. Then the familiar flip of her hair, and laughingly she said, "So, Carol. You want to come to a wedding?"

"You didn't come here to invite me to a wedding."

"No, I didn't. I came here to ask you to help me call off the wedding. I know I shouldn't marry this man. I also know what happens to me when I try not to see him."

"Did you feel better after you saw him?" I asked.

"Oh, yes. I felt great . . . until a friend of mine told me he saw him with Melanie."

"You have reason to believe him?"

"Yes, I believe him. He has no reason to lie to me."

"What did you do?"

"Nothing, really."

I noticed her whole body seemed to cave in under the weight of her thoughts. Now slightly slumped in the chair, she let out a huge sigh and said, "Look what happens to me when I try to get him out of my life. I become a degenerate. The only way I keep from killing myself is to masturbate to lingerie. I can't live without him unless I resort to a perverted compulsion. I'd say I'm in serious trouble. Wouldn't you agree?"

"Yes."

"Let's try this memory thing again. Whatever it is that I don't want to remember simply can't be as bad as the hell I'm living in now."

Thinking to myself that perhaps her recent experiences had shifted the balance of power, I answered, "You don't have much to lose by trying."

In the next session, we tried the backward association process again, but Hilary couldn't remember anything more than being afraid of some noises. She was feeling frustrated and discouraged. She was still seeing Sam because she was convinced that trying not to would be like going "cold turkey." And she hadn't called off the wedding, now less than five months away. "What do we do now, Carol?" she asked.

I thought we should try a memory link, so I asked her to bring in one of her lingerie items. I was hoping that by holding the item during a hypnotic trance, she would be more likely to recall her blocked memory.

Hilary arrived at the next session with nothing in hand. As soon as the door was shut behind us and both of us were seated, she said, "I brought it." Pointing to her over-size handbag, she added, "It's in my purse. I feel really stupid. Please reassure me this is going to help."

"I'm not sure it will work, but I think it's worth a try."

"So what do we do?"

"Put the lingerie in your lap, and then we'll get you into a relaxed state and see what happens."

She started to reach for her purse and then hesitated, leaning back in her chair instead. I could tell she was un-certain, scared of what might follow. She sat, momentarily staring out the window, once again twisting her hair around her fingers. Finally, with an audible sigh, she leaned forward, reached into her purse, and pulled out a cream-colored, silk teddy, which she dropped in her lap. Blush-ing, her eyes met mine and she resignedly said, "Now what?"

"Get comfortable, close your eyes, and take the five deep breaths as I count backward, Hilary. When you're feeling very relaxed, just signal me by raising a finger on your right hand." I waited for the signal, and when I saw her lift her finger, I said, "Pick up the lingerie, Hilary. Concentrate on it." She picked it up and in what seemed like an automatic motion, put it to her face, lightly rubbing the silk back and forth across her cheek. The action reminded me of a child who seeks comfort from a much-loved blanket. After a few moments I said, "Now tell me the first thing that comes to your mind."

"Tags." As she said this, I noticed for the first time that the item still had the store tag attached.

"What about the tags?" I asked.

"Lots of tags . . . all in a row."

"Where are the tags?"

"In a store . . . a lingerie department . . . there are rows
and rows of lingerie. I like to walk along and touch the tags
so that they are all dancing at the same time."

"How old are you, Hilary?"

"I'm all dressed up. I look very pretty." This last remark
was not that of a grown woman, but rather in the voice of
a little girl.

"Is someone noticing how pretty you look?"

A large smile appeared on her face as she answered in
her little-girl voice, "My daddy says I'm his beautiful little
princess. He tells me to pick out one of the lacy nighties. I
love to touch them and feel how soft they are against my
face. I like the pink ones and the purple ones best."

"Do you get to take the one you pick with you?"

Still in her little-girl voice, "Yes. Daddy buys it and then
we get it wrapped and I get to pick the wrapping paper and
the ribbon. I love to choose the ribbon. Each time I choose
a different-color ribbon."

"Each time?"

"Yes, Daddy and I do this lots."

"Where do you take the package, Hilary?"

As if it was suddenly burning her, she jerked the lingerie
away from her face and dropped it on the floor. Her smile
disappeared and was replaced by tight, pouting lips that
appeared to be fighting back something that wanted to be
revealed. "Can't tell. Daddy told me never to tell. It's our
secret."

I leaned over toward Hilary and softly and gently asked,
"What happens if you tell?"

"Daddy will be very angry . . . won't take me with him
anymore."

Still, very gently, "Did you ever tell?"

"No . . ." Then, in a tearful voice, "But Daddy stopped
taking me anyway."

"Why did he stop Hilary?"

"Nanny came back . . . didn't get to be his special princess anymore." Tears were now running down Hilary's closed eyes.

I let her cry for the moment while I gathered my thoughts. It was now clear to me that whatever transpired after the lingerie shopping was the crucial missing piece of the puzzle. I also knew that the little girl had effectively been silenced. It occurred to me that perhaps—just perhaps—the grown woman would not have to keep that promise made so many years before. I decided to give my theory a try. "Hilary, you're no longer a little girl. You're a grown woman now, and if you tell me where you and your father went after you went shopping, nothing bad will happen to you."

She didn't answer. Her face took on a puzzled look, as if she was considering what I had said. I waited for a short while and then repeated myself. "You're a grown woman now, Hilary. What you were afraid of then can't hurt you now. Nothing bad will happen to you if you tell."

I suspected from the various facial contortions she was experiencing that the two factions were fighting each other. All I could do was wait and see whether the scared little girl or the grown woman would win.

Suddenly, Hilary's eyes flew open and she bolted upright in the chair. Switching back to her adult voice she startled me by loudly screaming, "Goddamn him! How could he do that to me? I loved him, adored him." The screaming stopped and was replaced by a rasping voice that seemed more appropriate for the devil than for Hilary. "What a stupid, deceitful, hurtful thing for him to do." With a jerking motion, she reached down, picked up the lingerie, and began pulling and tearing at it. When she had succeeded in ripping it into several pieces, she threw it across the room. Her anger vented, she leaned forward in the chair with her head resting in her hands and cried. It was the kind of crying that comes from mixing incredible pain with incredible relief. Her crying came deep from within, building a momentum of its own until it was finally spent. When she was done crying, she lifted her head, sank back in the chair, and stared hard at me. After a few moments she literally spat out the words, ''I sure as hell hope you're going to tell me how remembering this is going to free me from my self-destructiveness.''

''I think it *will* free you, Hilary. Of course, you'll have to tell me what you remembered.''

She just looked at me, saying nothing. Behind that stare, I felt sure her mind was considering whether she could trust any other person with what she knew. Seconds passed and then she made the decision to tell me. Now back in control, she started talking in the cool, collected manner so familiar to me. ''After we went shopping, we would go to a hotel. Just the two of us would have dinner in the room, which was really a suite. You know, the kind that has a living room separate from the bedroom. After dinner we'd watch a little TV and I'd go to sleep on the couch in the living room. I remember how much I loved those Saturdays . . . until . . .'' She faltered, losing some of the control. Looking straight into my eyes, she was searching, I felt, for some reassurance that I would understand the pain of what she was about to tell me.

''It will be all right, Hilary. Letting go of your past pain will free you from your current pain.''

Her response was to sigh deeply. It was a sigh that I interpreted to mean she wasn't sure she believed me. So, when she continued, I was relieved. ''. . . Until I woke up once during the night.'' She stopped talking again and gazed out the window, as if she could find some answer written in the glass. Then she turned her eyes back to mine. Looking into her eyes, I was reminded of the sadness I had noticed the first day we met. I felt those eyes calling to me, begging for salvation from the painful memory. Now in control again, she continued in an emotionless monotone, ''I must have had a bad dream. I woke up afraid and, at first, didn't know where I was. Then I remembered my father was in the other room. I felt frightened and wanted to be with him. I could see light coming from underneath the door, so I walked over to the door. As I got closer, I could hear voices in the room. At first I thought it was the TV, but then I heard a woman say my name. I slowly opened the door just enough to peek in. The wrappings from the package were on the floor. A woman was standing next to the bed. I could feel a shooting pain in my heart as I became aware of the fact that she was wearing the lingerie I had picked out. She was saying, 'It's risky what we're doing. We'd never be able to explain this to her if she woke up and discovered us.' Then my father answered back, 'I've told you before not to worry about her. She's slept through earthquakes. Forget her and come to me.' Then I watched with horror as she climbed into the bed and I saw my father putting his hands all over her. She was moaning and wiggling her body. I wanted to die . . . yet I couldn't take my eyes off the two of them. There he was . . . with another woman . . . she wasn't even pretty.'' As soon as she said the last sentence, she knew. She started laughing, a strange demonic laugh. ''Of course. Sam's just like *him*. He says I make him happy, and then he betrays me with another woman. This is the unfinished business you talked about, isn't it?''

With Hilary's memory of this traumatic event came the explanation for her obsession. It wasn't Sam so much as the situation that Hilary was obsessed by. Sam's infidelity was like her father's infidelity. Hilary was driven to make this situation have a different ending than the one with her father. She would stay with Sam until he chose her over the other woman. In Hilary's mind, there was no other alternative.

''Sam has the same characteristics as your father,'' I answered back. "He's charming, successful, dishonest, and a womanizer. Your conscious mind didn't recognize the reincarnation of your father, but your unconscious did. You're trying for a second chance. Only this time you're determined to win."

"So, I'm trying to get Sam to pick me over Melanie so I can stop feeling the rejection I felt as a result of seeing my father with that woman?"

"Yes. But do you remember us talking about how your unconscious is trying to protect you?"

"I remember us talking about that. I wasn't sure I understood what you meant by it."

"Well, your unconscious wants to give you a second chance to learn an important lesson. However, the lesson is not how to compete with other women in order to feel loved. What you're really getting is an opportunity to feel deserving of an honest, loyal man. Once you feel entitled to that, you'll pick someone who'll treat you the way you deserve to be treated. You won't have to compete. Winning or losing simply won't be an issue."

"I get it . . . fall in love with the good ones, not the lousy ones. But to do that I have to like myself—believe I'm worth it." She paused for a moment as if mulling over this last thought, then said, "So, what happens next? Am I going to be able to dump Sam and not feel a thing? Will I go home, pack up all the lingerie, and give it away? Am I cured?"

"I don't know. I think you ought to spend some time with Sam and see how you feel."

"Spend time with Sam? I didn't expect you to say that. And, you know, it's interesting, Carol, all of a sudden, the idea of spending time with him doesn't seem that pleasant. But neither does the idea of ending it. Mostly, I guess I feel numb."

"It takes time to heal, Hilary. Experiment. Be with him. See what happens and how you feel about being with him."

Hilary called me a few days prior to our next session to tell me she would be out of town filming a movie. She said she'd be gone for a few weeks but would call me to reschedule when she got back in town. When I asked how she was doing, she was hesitant. "I'm still feeling numb. I've seen Sam only once, just for dinner, and I felt pretty much nothing. But I do feel I can manage a few weeks without him. I'll know more after I try to put back the pieces of my career. I screwed up last time and can't afford to turn this opportunity down."

Although I was glad to see Hilary feeling up to working again, I didn't like the idea of her missing sessions at this point. She'd been through a lot, and unearthing buried ghosts rarely creates instant, miracle cures; life rarely changes dramatically. It takes time to absorb insights, to integrate them into thought processes so you arrive at different conclusions. It's not so much the insight that is curative, but rather the conclusions one makes as a result of the insight. Conclusions are what determine behavior. Thus, my attempt to steer Hilary toward the conclusion that her second chance was about valuing herself to fall in love with good, loyal men—men unlike her father.

There was another reason I felt uncomfortable about her postponing sessions at this time. I was concerned about a part of the story I thought Hilary left out, maybe intentionally, maybe not. Her erotic attachment to the lingerie still puzzled me. A strong erotic attachment to a specific item usually comes from having experienced sexual arousal in the presence of the object during early sexual development. Although Hilary hadn't mentioned it, I suspected that, in addition to feeling rejection at the sight of her father with the woman, she also felt sexually aroused. Of course, being so young, she would have been unable to identify the feelings as erotic. Nonetheless, the association was likely to have been firmly implanted in her mind in the form of imagery. This imagery would later surface as a repetitive fantasy in which the object had to be present in order for sexual arousal to occur. So, in Hilary's case, the lingerie needed to be present in order for her to get aroused, both with Sam and masturbation. There was a revenge part of Hilary's fantasy as well. She wanted to hurt her father—to punish him for breaking her heart. So, in her fantasy, she leaves him and he experiences the rejection—not her. This would explain the pained expression on the man's face as she's walking out on him.

Over the years, I've encountered numerous people who have made such early erotic attachments to different objects or people. Almost always, even though they are too young to articulate the feelings as erotic, there is still great guilt and shame associated with the feelings. The guilt and shame are responsible for sending the whole erotic experience underground—out of sight, out of mind, so to speak. As I mentioned earlier, the erotic part of the personality refuses to be completely swept under the rug. Instead, in an attempt to rescue eroticism from total oblivion, the eroticism reappears in a perverted form.

I felt fairly sure my hypothesis was correct. But I wasn't the one who needed to understand this association, and I wasn't sure Hilary was ready to face another intensely painful realization. Once again, however, it wasn't up to me to make the decision about her readiness. Oftentimes, life's circumstances force the issue. I simply had to wait and see in what direction Hilary's life would go.

When she got back from filming, she did call me for an appointment. In that session and several to follow, we talked mostly about Sam. Briefly, this is what transpired. When she returned from out of town, she was feeling brave. Her work had gone well and she was feeling good about herself. So, she challenged Sam's ultimatum and called off the wedding. He was furious. "That's it," he said, and slammed the door on his way out. Hilary thought he would call when he calmed down. He didn't.

It wasn't easy for her but she survived this period. She was able to sleep at night and do normal things during the day. There were many times she felt shaky and wanted to call him, but somehow she managed to keep from dialing his number. She was feeling fairly proud of herself for resisting the temptation. Just as she was feeling stronger, he called, saying he thought they could work it out if they both really tried. She decided to see him, she maintained, just to satisfy her curiosity—to see how she would feel. After all, didn't I tell her to experiment with her feelings? What she discovered was that it didn't feel the same as before. It didn't feel bad, but it didn't feel good either.

Hilary said she liked this neutral place. It gave her a feeling of being more in control, a more comfortable feeling. Then everything turned upside down again. I received a frantic, early-morning call shortly after our last session. Could I see her immediately? I could sense the desperation in her voice and agreed to make room for her that day. When she arrived in my office, she looked like anything but the typical Hilary. She was wearing jeans, the same old sweatshirt, and not a speck of makeup. But what really told me she was in trouble was her hair. She hadn't bothered to put a comb through it, and it looked like a tangled bird's nest. Hilary seemed undaunted by her disheveled appearance. Instead, she paced back and forth in my office, talking nonstop.

"You know how I was feeling pretty good last time I was here? Well, that certainly didn't last. As soon as Sam started pressing me for sex . . . well . . . I just fell apart. He said he couldn't stand being without me. He missed our Saturday soirees and wanted to take me shopping for lingerie. It was as if he knew my vulnerability. You know, hit me where I'm weak so I'll give in. Well, I refused to go. We had a spat about it, and once again Sam left in a fury.

"Later, he shows up at my door with a package. I went

crazy when I saw the package. I was flooded with the entire memory of my dad and that woman. I was repulsed, angry, almost hysterical and . . . wildly turned on. I couldn't believe this response was coming from me. How could I possibly be feeling sexually aroused by such a horrible memory? It was so unreal. I felt incredibly weak, unable to resist opening the package even though I knew what would be inside. Of course, Sam wanted me to put the lingerie on.'' She paused here for the first time. She looked at me, then looked away, evidently struggling with the decision to go on. Then she took a seat but remained on the edge of the chair, as if to make a quick getaway if she needed to. Finally she resumed her monologue. ''It was as if my body was acting independent of my mind . . . .'' Now her voice was cracking. ''I did what he asked. It turned me on even more. Then we had the most fantastic sex. I mean the orgasms . . . and I mean orgasms—with an s—went on and on.

''Afterwards, I can't remember ever feeling such torment. I cried hysterically. Sam was dumbfounded by my tears. He kept asking me what was wrong. I couldn't tell him. All I could do was cry. Finally, I cried myself to sleep. When I woke the next morning and saw Sam in my bed, I became hysterical all over again. I was miserable from the guilt I felt. I kept asking myself how I could do such a thing. I wanted to die and even thought about killing myself. I actually went into the bathroom to see if I had enough sleeping pills to do it. Fortunately, I didn't. I don't know, Carol, what I would have done if I did have enough pills . . . that's when I called you. . . . What the hell is happening to me, Carol? Am I ever going to be free of this perverted sexual attachment I have to lingerie?''

''I think you will understand what's happening to you if we go back again in time to the night you saw your father with the other woman. Close your eyes again and re-create the scene. Tell me out loud what you're seeing.''

Hilary repeated the scene as she had before. When she got to the part where her father began touching the other woman, she hesitated. A pained expression crossed her face, and her body tightened. ''Tell me what you're seeing and feeling,'' I said.

''I'm feeling . . . I'm feeling . . . I can't tell you what I'm feeling. It's too confusing.''

''Then you're feeling confused?''

''Yes! I'm feeling so bad, but I'm feeling good too.''

''Good?''

''Well, it's a warm feeling in my body . . . I feel like . . . like I'm going to wet my pants. I try to hold it back. I don't wet my pants, but the hot feeling doesn't go away. It's scary, but it feels good. Then I run back to the couch and start touching myself between my legs and my whole body is flooded with the warm, good feeling.'' Hilary opened her eyes, blinking several times as she tried to bring herself back to the present. Then she sat up in the chair and said, ''I had an orgasm, didn't I? Is that possible? I was only a child.''

''Yes, it's possible. And you're exactly right. You were only a child, Hilary. A very innocent child. But you've never forgiven yourself. You've been carrying that shame with you all these years. You repressed the memory, hoping to rid yourself of the shame.''

''What I don't understand is how the lingerie fits in to this sordid picture''

''Why do you say 'sordid'?''

''It's disgusting. A four-year-old child being turned on by watching her daddy in bed with a woman.''

''Hilary, you were just a child, responding to normal sexual urges. It's not disgusting. It's just innocent sexual feelings. You're not to blame for responding the way you did.''

''It's absurd. Four-year-olds don't have 'normal' sexual feelings.''

''Why not?''

''I've never heard of such a thing.''

''It's very real, Hilary. It's just that the thought of a child having sexual urges makes most adults very uncomfortable. To keep from being uncomfortable, adults collude with each other in pretending it doesn't exist. When a child feels something that isn't supposed to exist, it creates shame. That's why you feel so much shame for being aroused by the scene you witnessed.''

''You told me before that if I could stop feeling so guilty about these feelings, I would no longer be addicted to this lingerie thing. Is that really the way it works?''

''Think of the guilt as the fuel that feeds the entire process. The guilt causes you to blame yourself, Hilary. As a result you feel like a bad girl, undeserving of a good man. If you can forgive yourself for feeling aroused, you'll stop feeling guilty, and then you'll feel deserving of a good relationship.''

''But how does the lingerie fit into all of this?''

''The warm, good, sexual feeling you had is tied up in your mind with the lingerie. You loved being with your dad, shopping for the beautiful, lacy nighties. The lingerie shopping trips also gave you a warm, good feeling. The two feelings felt the same for you. So the erotic feelings you had when you witnessed the sexual scene became associated with the lingerie. At four, you couldn't identify the feeling as erotic so you identified the lingerie as bringing on the feeling.''

Hilary sat staring at me for a moment, a puzzled look on her face. Then, as if a light bulb had gone off in her head, she said, ''I know someone who was once terrified of cats. He couldn't even be in a room with a cat without breaking out in a sweat. When he went into therapy, he discovered that when he very young, he had witnessed a terrible fight between his parents. His father got so angry he hit his mother. She fell backwards, landing on the cat who, in turn, ran out of the room and right into him. Frightened, the cat acted as if he was the enemy and scratched him badly. Until therapy, he didn't remember anything at all about the incident. All he knew was that he was deathly afraid of cats. . . . It's the same thing . . . what you're saying about me and the lingerie, right?''

''Right. By the way, did your friend get over being afraid of cats?''

Hilary smiled. The smile seemed to transform her once again into the beautiful goddess I first met, and I imagined I saw some of the sadness in those big brown eyes lift as she said, ''Yes, he did. In fact, he even owns a cat now.''

MITCH

RENTED LOVE

There was a sameness to Mitch's life; a sameness born of routine and rigidity. It didn't matter if it was a Tuesday or a Sunday, each day looked exactly like the last. It was a kind of prison existence that would drive most people crazy—yet it was Mitch's link to sanity.

Any outsider who peered into Mitch's life would have been quick to label him weird. Knowing this, Mitch didn't let any outsiders into his life. He lived alone, ate alone, and slept alone. He claimed he liked his eccentricity; he didn't want to be like anybody else. It was only after I knew him well that I came to understand how he hid behind his uniqueness as a defense against his fear of conformity. For Mitch, nonconformity gave him an identity; being different set him apart from others, whereas conformity meant oblivion.

In the beginning of our relationship he wore his alien behavior as if it were a shield of armor, deflecting any attempts I made to get to know him. There was one way, however, in which Mitch didn't want to be different from other men: He wanted to have sex with a woman. It was desperation for sex with a woman, not his ritualistic life-style, that drove him to seek therapy. At thirty-five, Mitch had never been sexual with a woman. He had never kissed or touched a woman's body. In fact, Mitch had never even been on a date with a woman. Although the rest of his odd life seemed acceptable to Mitch, he detested the fact that he was still a virgin.

Of course, on the day we met, I knew none of this. What I did sense upon meeting him was that fashion was definitely not his forte. He wore a pair of loose-fitting, khaki-colored trousers that were too short at the ankles, thus drawing attention to dingy white socks that literally spilled over worn-out tennis shoes that in turn supported a medium-height, slightly paunchy frame. A light-blue, long-sleeved, button-down shirt, frayed at the collar, was covered by a black nylon jacket. He wore his hair short, the kind of short you're willing to forgive only in new military recruits. And he wore glasses, thick, heavy-framed, black, Buddy Holly–type glasses. From a distance he looked more like a kid in his teens than a man in his thirties. Up close, however, his skin revealed his age. His face was covered with the battle scars of the proverbial adolescent war with acne. Just looking at Mitch, I immediately knew that his biography would contain the hurtful social punishment reserved for the unattractive.

I was further convinced of my supposition when we shook hands. His hand was clammy, his grip limp, and, rather than look me in the eyes, he focused just to the right of me. He shifted his weight nervously as we introduced ourselves and continued to shift his body around even after being seated.

It's difficult to feel connected to someone who won't look you in the eye. So, without a word being spoken, I felt I already knew something important about Mitch: Making human connections was not easy for him. This notion fit with my previous assumption that he was socially uncomfortable and had probably experienced a great deal of pain from being a social outcast. After I was introduced to his distracting habit of constantly shifting in his chair as if searching for a more comfortable position, I wondered if this behavior didn't serve as a metaphor for his life.

Then, because I incorrectly assumed that lack of social grace would go hand-in-hand with shyness, I was taken aback at his straightforwardness when he first spoke. "I'm thirty-five and still a virgin. And don't go thinking I'm gay because I'm not. I just want to get laid."

This last comment was said with such determination that had he been looking into my eyes rather than at the wall behind me, I might have taken the remark as a direct challenge for me to produce his seducer. But instinct told me Mitch wasn't in my office because he thought sex therapists were procurers. Rather, he was here to make a plea for salvation from a yet-undisclosed pain. His plea was indirect and disguised, but nonetheless beseeching.

At the time, I had no idea about the degree of Mitch's social isolation, so I responded to his statement with a question. "Is there someone you have in mind?" As soon as I asked it, I realized it might sound mocking so I quickly added, "I mean a girlfriend?"

"No, I don't have a girlfriend. Never have had a girlfriend. Don't care for 'em much. Girls want things from you, you know, they tell you what to do, how to live your life. They want to change you. I don't want to be changed. I just want to have sex."

"If you don't want a relationship . . ."

"I know what you're thinking," he interrupted. "Why don't I just find a prostitute? Well, prostitutes aren't safe. I want sex, but not badly enough to risk getting AIDS. And I hate singles bars."

I wasn't thinking about prostitutes at all. But Mitch had offered me more valuable information. Obviously, he was

informed about the current dangers of multiple sex partners. He might be rough in his presentation, but his last
comment told me not to assume he was unsophisticated
and uninformed about sex. I was also interested in his bla-
tant rejection of singles bars so I asked, "What is it you
don't like about the bars?"

"Most of the chicks are dogs, and the pretty ones won't
give you the time of day. You know, they give you that 'get
lost' look, as if the merchandise says 'look but don't
touch.' "

I felt a tremendous sadness as the irony of Mitch's words
hit me. Here was a man who, from purely external appear-
ances, would himself be considered a "dog" (if that term
weren't solely reserved for women), yet his unattractiveness
did not exempt him from being indoctrinated as much as
any man to desire physical beauty in a woman. I had known
this man for less than five minutes and once again I was
struck with the same thought: His pain from social rejection
must be very strong. His situation was a sure setup for
rejection: an unattractive man who lusts only for beautiful
women. What was his actual experience with rejection? I
wondered. "Have you ever tried to approach a woman you
were attracted to and been told to get lost?" I asked him.

"No. Like I said, I hate singles bars so I don't go much."

"Have you ever approached a woman in any place besides a singles bar?"

"No."

Now curious as to where he thought he might meet
women, I asked, "So, where do you spend your free time?"

"At home mostly."

"It's pretty difficult to meet women if you stay at home.
What about work? Are there any interesting women at your
work?"

"I'm a computer programmer. I spend time with computers. I change them—they don't change me," he snick-
ered.

This was the second time he mentioned the issue of being

changed. Each time there was contempt in his voice. This was a big issue for Mitch and one that I felt certain would be raised again and again. Right now, however, I wanted to do a little reality testing. How did he think he was going to have sex with a woman with the obstacles he was placing in his way? He isolated himself socially, ruled out the possibilities of prostitutes, and wouldn't put himself on the line by risking a pickup. I needed to know more about what was going on inside his head. ''Why do you think you're still a virgin, Mitch?'' I asked.

''Because I haven't met a pretty girl.''

''Where do you think other men meet pretty women?''

''It just happens.''

''It just happens?''

''Well, that's the way it happens in the movies.''

''What movies?''

''All of them. You see, I rent a lot of movies. Guys are always meeting gorgeous women in the movies. It's easy. They don't have to *do* anything. The women go after them and pretty soon they're rolling around in the hay.''

''And real life is like the movies?''

''Sure. I know this guy at work. He's married, but he has women after him all the time. He's always talking about getting laid. Last week he says he was out in his driveway working on his car and this babe walks by and starts talking to him. Next thing you know he's made this date with her to meet her at a hotel. Just like that.'' Mitch gave a snap of his fingers to emphasize his point.

My mind was trying to assimilate everything Mitch was telling me. He avoids women because he believes they want to control him, or worse, because they will reject him. His fantasy, obviously fueled by movies, is that they will come to him on his terms: He won't have to *do* anything to get them and then he can discard them when he's done. That way there's no rejection and no controlling him. This last thought made me wonder what role movies played in his life.

95

A recent discussion I had about nonviolent pornography with Warren Farrell, the author of *Why Men Are the Way They Are*, came to mind. He told me he believed all men are literally drugged by 10 million images a year of beautiful women. According to Farrell, this creates an obsession in which the average male thinks about sex maybe six times an hour. But the reality is that the average male only has sex about once a week. The discrepancy between the desire and the reality is filled by fantasy. Farrell suggested that pornography, which is one form of fantasy, is often used to fill the gap. Pornography, he said, gives men access to a variety of attractive women without fear of rejection and at a price they can afford. I remembered something in particular that Farrell had said that most likely applied to Mitch. He had said that unattractive men are more likely than attractive men to use this this type of fantasy because they have less access to beautiful women.

This is exactly the irony I sensed in Mitch's life. Given Mitch's lack of social grace and style, he was bound to have little access to beautiful women. Of course this would create an even stronger need. This is exactly the kind of situation that can be dangerous because it sets up an additional scarcity of supply in an area where demand is naturally high. I say dangerous in the sense that otherwise ordinary people will act in erratic ways when their need is great but they're denied access to a limited supply. In Mitch's case, it was likely that he was doing exactly what Farrell had suggested: resorting to pornography to satisfy his unmet need.

My concern was that with Mitch, pornography was more than filling a gap. The use of pornography is widespread among men. Some use it only occasionally as a supplement to partner sex. Others use it compulsively as a substitute for partner sex. These men have extreme difficulty relating sexually to real people. Pornography allows them to satisfy their erotic urges without the anxiety that comes from forming an intimately bonding relationship.

The use of pornography is very misunderstood in our culture. Many people think that it is the use of pornography that creates sexual deviations and sexual offenders. This is not the case. Sexual abnormalities are created as a result of guilty feelings about sexual urges. Guilty feelings predominate in an environment where sexual learning and sexual rehearsal play in childhood is forbidden and/or punished. When there are a lot of guilty or bad feelings attached to sexual urges, the person creates a splitting between love and sex. Sexual feelings are not permitted toward someone who is respected and loved. Pornography usurps the loved one.

But I was getting ahead of myself. Mitch might not be one of those individuals who is unable to feel sexual toward someone he loves. I needed to know much more about his use of the movies and about his childhood. That would come in time. Right now Mitch was talking about how his friend had such easy access to women. I wanted to know more about his thought processes. What mental manipulations was he performing in his head to deal with this unmet need he had? "Why do you think your friend at work has so many women?" I asked.

"He's not really my friend. Friends I don't need . . . . I just listen to him talk all the time. Things happen to him just like they do in the movies. I want what he seems to be able to get. He doesn't even have to try."

"Tell me about the kind of woman you want to have sex with."

"Tall, long blonde hair, great body, with fantastic legs and a big chest. They always have a big chest in the movies."

"Are these X-rated movies?"

"Some of them . . . well, most of them."

"Do you get turned on when you're watching the movies?"

For a split second his eyes made contact with mine, but

they immediately darted once again toward the wall behind me where they had been fixed for practically the whole session. Hesitantly, he answered, "Yeah. I get turned on."

I knew the next question always created an embarrassing response so I asked as matter-of-factly as I could, "Do you masturbate to the movies, Mitch?"

"Sure. What's wrong with that?"

"Did you think I was implying it was wrong?"

"Well, most people think it's bad. You know, perverted."

"Did anyone ever specifically tell you it was bad?"

"Sure. I went to Catholic schools. Masturbation is a sin. You get told that enough times and you get to feeling pretty creepy about doing it. I remember as a kid feeling terrible afterward. You know, like I was going to be punished somehow. I'd tell myself I'd never do it again . . . but, of course, I did. I mean I couldn't seem to stop."

"What about now, Mitch? Does it still feel like you can't stop?"

"Yeah. It feels that way. That's why I decided I need to get laid. I know if I could just be normal in the sex department, you know, like other men, I wouldn't need to masturbate so much."

"What is 'so much'?"

Again, he gave me a brief moment of direct eye contact before he mumbled, "Couple times a day." He was silent for a moment, as if struggling with the next thought. Finally, he said, "On the weekends I do it a lot. Maybe three or four times a day." He seemed to relax a little after saying this—almost as if his confession was over with and now the pressure was off. Then, perhaps because he was feeling less pressure, he said, "I've never seen a therapist before. I didn't know what to expect."

"Do you know why you've decided to see one now?"

"The guys at work think I'm gay because I never participate in their bragging sessions. I'm tired of them always telling their stories and laughing. Sometimes I think they're laughing at me. Besides, my parents are always putting pressure on me because I never go out with girls. They keep wanting to fix me up with the daughters of their friends. My dad's never said anything to me, but I just know he's afraid I might be gay. That scares the shit out of him. I know I'm not gay, but I know that masturbating four or five times a day isn't what I want to do for the rest of my life. If I just have sex with a woman, even once, then I'd be normal and wouldn't need to jerk off . . . uh . . . sorry about that. Hope you're not insulted.''

''I'm not insulted.''

''Good, because I'm sure I'll forget sometimes and say things . . . well, you know what I mean.''

''Yes, I know what you mean.''

It didn't take long for his therapy hour to be ''programmed,'' like everything else, into Mitch's life. He never once asked to change the day or time of his session. Without fail, he arrived five minutes early—never six or four—always five minutes early. While in the waiting room, he paced back and forth rather than having a seat. During our sessions he fidgeted in his chair, sometimes getting up, walking around the room, and then returning to the chair. His dress rarely varied: ill-fitting khaki pants, grayish-white socks, beat-up tennis shoes, light-blue shirt, and black nylon jacket.

As I learned more about Mitch over the next months, I came to realize that, although there was much about him that was predictable, there was little about him that was typical. Except for his work, Mitch lived a totally reclusive and regimented life. He woke up at exactly the same time every morning and masturbated before getting out of bed. He drove exactly the same route home every evening, stopping in video stores on the way. He selected only one type of movie: boy meets girl, boy gets girl, boy dumps girl. It didn't always have to be pornographic to have this story line, but pornography was a guarantee of this theme. So Mitch watched both kinds. It didn't matter to him that after a while, he saw the same films over and over again.

On the weekends, when he wasn't watching movies, he spent time at his computer. He was developing a highly technical software program that could track traffic patterns throughout the city. He predicted that cars would eventually be equipped with computer screens connected to a main terminal. His software would allow a person to program his destination and then see on the screen the open and closed routes, depending on traffic flow at any given moment. There was no question that Mitch had a gifted, but limited, brilliance. Over the years, he had learned how to retreat into that brilliance to avoid interacting with people.

Except to go the grocery store and have his weekly dinners with his parents, Mitch didn't go out and didn't have anyone over. He had a telephone in his apartment but claimed he never used it. He got it, he said, because his boss sometimes needed to reach him and because it made his parents more comfortable.

Mitch insisted he was content with his predictable, isolated life. People introduced complications, he said, especially women. He felt sure that if he had a regular girlfriend in his life, he wouldn't be able to spend time at his computer on the weekends. No, he was sure he didn't want a girlfriend—just a woman to have sex with and then send on her way. He liked his isolation because it allowed him to be totally in control of his life.

I was intrigued by the way in which Mitch was able to find comfort in his peculiar life and yet find great discomfort in his "abnormal" virginal status. To him, the two seemed separate issues. He kept emphasizing to me that he didn't want to change his ritualistic life, only his sexual status. Although he kept saying to me over and over again, "I just want to be normal," he meant that in a very restricted way.

As our sessions continued, I tried to point out the inconsistency in his thinking. Mitch said he wanted to have sex. But he was also trying to escape the reality of possible rejection. He had placed himself between two opposing forces. To have sex with a woman, he'd have to get close enough to one to touch her. That would make her real, not a fantasy. No wonder he was thirty-five and still a virgin. The conflict between these two forces kept him at an impasse. Yet every time I attempted to approach the discrepancy in his thinking, he responded by retreating to his fantasy world.

"How do you expect to meet women if you stay home, Mitch?" I'd ask.

"In the movies, women go after men," he'd answer.

"Life isn't always like the movies," I'd answer back.

"Yes it is. The guy at work gets women just like in the movies."

"What's this guy like?" I'd ask.

"About fifty, potbellied, and balding," he told me. "And he doesn't have money either so I know it's not just because he can buy women."

By this time, I was convinced that Mitch was socially phobic. His anxiety about being rejected by others was creating a fear of interaction with people outside his regulated work routine. Social phobia first appears in early adolescence but becomes extremely serious by the age of seventeen or eighteen. Its roots are still undetermined and may be multiple; it could be a combination of inherited shyness and a series of bad experiences of being rejected; it could be learned at home; or it could be a part of a deeper psychological constellation. Mitch was dealing with his fear by denial and by retreating into a fantasy world. He would probably have been comfortable with these coping mechanisms were it not for the virginal part.

Several months went by and we weren't moving anywhere. I knew I needed to take a different tack, but I wasn't sure where to go. Then, an incident occurred that lowered his defensive shield and propelled us forward in the therapeutic process. It happened on a Sunday evening, his usual time to have dinner with his parents. Until this incident, Mitch steadfastly insisted that his childhood had nothing to do with his current situation. He resisted delving into his past. "I had a normal childhood," he would tell me. "I didn't date in high school, but then I never wanted to, so it wasn't a big deal," was all he would say.

But the Sunday evening in question changed his belief that his childhood hadn't influenced his current behavior. He arrived at his parents at exactly 7:00 P.M., his usual time. But when he drove up to the house he saw a strange car parked in the driveway, blocking his usual parking place. He was upset by having to alter his normal routine and also puzzled as to whose car it was.

When he went inside, he found, seated on the sofa, a young woman, perhaps thirty years old, whom he'd never seen before. His father was sitting across from her, and they were talking. When his father saw him come in the door, he stood and walked over to him.

"Mitch, I want you to meet Janet," he said. "She's just moved here from Atlanta. Her mother is a friend of your mother's. Since Janet didn't know anybody out here, your mom thought it would be nice for the two of you to meet."

Mitch glared at his father. He could see beads of sweat forming on his father's upper lip, signaling his anxiety. This was the first time his parents had gone against his wishes about fixing him up. His father obviously wanted it to go well. He was just trying to help. All of these thoughts flashed through his mind and still he was furious. He wanted to turn around and walk out the door. The girl was plain and small-breasted, not like the women he saw in the movies. He could never be turned on by her. Why did his parents think he would be interested in a girl like this?

Mitch felt the room closing in on him. How would he get through the evening? If he stayed, he would have to talk to her. He didn't have anything to say to her. He could tell by looking at her that she knew nothing about computers. He felt unable to talk and his head was starting to spin.

The awkwardness in the room hung like a thick fog. Finally, Janet got up from the sofa and walked over to Mitch. She put out her hand and said, "Hi, it's nice to meet you. I guess they didn't tell you I was coming."

"No, they didn't." He hadn't planned on being nice to her but she had caught him off guard. Next thing he knew he was saying, "But it's all right. I'm glad you're here." Then he put out his hand to shake hers. He could hear his father breathe a sigh of relief.

In the session following this incident, Mitch was more agitated than ever. As usual there was little eye contact, and he paced the floor as he told me about the evening. "This Janet chick and I shook hands. It was really weird. I don't remember ever shaking hands with a girl. Her hand felt strange, you know, kind of warm and soft. I liked it but I didn't like it.

"Just then my mother came into the room and she was wearing this apron she always wears when she cooks. I mean, she's worn this apron for years. Now, all of a sudden for some reason I hate the apron. I'm thinking she should have gotten rid of it years ago. It makes her look like an old hag. I feel really pissed at her. It's so weird, I mean, I'm used to feeling irritated at her. She's always been nosy, asking me personal questions that are none of her business. And she hovers too much. You know, always hanging around me. She's like a bee that keeps buzzing around a flower. Even after my sister was born . . . I was nine at the time . . . I thought she'd have something else to do besides get in my way. No such luck. She just kept hovering.

"Anyway, I'm always a little irritated by her, but that night Janet was there, well, now I'm more than irritated, I'm pissed. Of course, I was angry at both of them for inviting Janet. But I really felt much angrier with Mom. So anyway, she starts to walk over to the three of us. And I know she's going to try to hug me. She always hugs me when she sees me. I hate it. God, I hate it when she does that. It feels suffocating. I mean, I let her do it because if I say anything about it, she'll cry, but I can't stand it when she hugs me. Never have liked her to do that.

"So, anyway. I get through the evening. Of course, I don't say much during dinner. Everybody's uncomfortable. Mom and Dad and this Janet chick are trying to make small talk. Really dumb-shit stuff. This Janet, well, she's not ugly but she didn't turn me on. Too skinny and, like I said, no boobs on her. I want a girl with big knockers." His hands went out in front of his chest to reinforce the picture.

"Anyway, you're always asking me questions about my mom and dad so I thought you'd want to hear this story." Then something unusual happened. Mitch stopped pacing and looked me in the eyes. "Why do you think I got so angry with Mom?" he asked.

There it was. A glimmer of interest from Mitch. In all the months we had worked together, Mitch had never shown the slightest interest in what his behavior might mean beyond its superficial and obvious purpose. He had never once asked "Why?" When I asked him why he did something he always gave a simplistic answer. For example, I'd ask, "Why do you think you rent those movies, Mitch?" "Why not? Nothing else to do," he'd answer.

Now here he was, standing in front of me, actually looking me in the eyes and asking "Why?" It was just a start, but an important one. He was lowering his guard and taking the risk of learning something about himself. I was fascinated by his question. Out of the whole story, the part he was most curious about was the angry reaction he had toward his mother. He didn't know it, but he was revealing valuable information that would eventually help him get what he wanted. " I think you've been angry with your mom for a long time," I replied.

"You do? Why is that?"

There it was again. Not only did he not deny my supposition, but he was willing to ask for an interpretation.

"Well, it's just a supposition, Mitch, but I think your negative feelings about women originated with your mom."

"You know, you keep doing that."

"Doing what?"

"Trying to get me to say bad things about my mom."

Mitch was circling the wagons again—putting up his defenses. His defensiveness convinced me more than ever that his relationship with his mother played an important role in his need to distance himself from women. True, he wasn't yet ready to face this possibility. The glimmer was just that, a glimmer, now faded to black. Still, I was thrilled at the light, however momentary, that was thrown on our sessions. I knew we had made a breakthrough and that we'd move forward. Therapy is like that. It's rarely linear. Rather, if plotted on a graph, it would have peaks and valleys, but its overall movement would be upward.

"It's not that I want you to say bad things, Mitch. It's just that I believe that all of us make assumptions about what men and women are like based on how we perceive our parents to be."

"Well, I told you. I get irritated with my mom because she gets in my space. But she's an okay person."

"It's just that you've told me you don't want a girlfriend because she'd get in your space too. I saw some similarities in what you were saying about your mom and about girlfriends." I was watching Mitch carefully, hoping that this last comment would not be so threatening that he would close down even further. I was glad he didn't respond right away because that meant he was thinking about what I said.

"I never thought about that before. You're saying girls remind me of my mom."

"It's one possibility, Mitch."

"What other possibilities do you see?"

He was opening himself up again. He was asking for another interpretation. This was a good sign. I knew I had to be careful, though. He could easily retreat. Move it away from the personal, I thought. Talk in generalities. That would be less threatening. Let *him* personalize it. "You've told me your interest in women is limited to your being sexual with them. Is that right?"

"Yeah, that's right."

"Well, I've found that men who feel this way have usually had a lot of rejection from a woman or perhaps several women."

"I've never been that interested in getting to know any women so I don't remember experiencing any rejection."

"Any idea why you never had any interest?"

"No. Computers seemed more interesting, I guess."

He was retreating again—reverting back to his tendency to see his behavior as one-dimensional. It's a powerful defense because there's some truth to it. It's difficult to get someone who uses this one-dimensional tactic to accept that motivations exist on several different levels. It was true that Mitch received satisfaction from using his "technological" mind. His genius in this area was rewarding rather than rejecting so it was natural for him to gravitate toward something that made him feel good about himself. But this was as far as he got in his thinking. He couldn't see that he turned off the other parts of his personality, which didn't bring him the same satisfaction. Part of the reason he found computers more interesting than women was because he felt women wouldn't find him interesting. It's another version of the "I'll leave you before you leave me" type of thinking. How long had he felt this way? I wondered. "You don't remember ever having an interest in girls? Even in grade school?"

"There was this girl about my age in the neighborhood. We used to play together."

"How old were you?"

"Let's see . . . we were living on Rawlins Street then so it must have been the summer after the sixth grade."

"Did you like her?"

"Yeah, but her parents wouldn't let her play with me after a while."

"Why was that?"

"Something happened."

"Can you tell me about it, Mitch?"

"It wasn't much. I was trying to kiss her and she kept pushing me away, so I held her down. She started to cry and her mother came in the room and got real mad at me. Her mother called my parents. I can't remember too well, but they must have been mad too because they sent me away to a summer camp. I do remember not wanting to go to that stupid camp. All they did at that dumb camp was sports. I don't like sports much either."

"You think they sent you to camp because of that incident with the girl?"

"My mom said it would be the best thing because the girl's parents were really upset. She said they'd be over it by the time I got back."

"Maybe the girl's parents thought you were doing more than trying to kiss her?"

"Yeah, I thought about that later. Maybe that's why they got so mad, huh?" Mitch was quiet for a moment, and then in an uncharacteristically doleful tone of voice said, "But I wasn't. She was so pretty. I just wanted to give her a kiss."

The usual hardness in Mitch's face disappeared for a moment and was replaced by a sadness that revealed, for the first time since I'd met him, a certain vulnerability. I thought about the impact this experience must have had on him. It had been an innocent attempt to give a neighborhood girl a simple kiss. Not only had he experienced rejection by the girl, but he had been sent away for his overtures. Sending him off to camp had seemed like a punishment. In his mind, that would make his amorous attempts a crime. Obviously, the incident had left its mark on him.

It's possible that one such incident could create a severe case of social phobia, especially if there is a preexisting sensitivity to rejection. I still felt, however, that Mitch's earlier years with his mother held some clues to that preexisting sensitivity. It had been his recognition of his anger at his mother that had lowered some of his defenses and opened him up. I felt certain that his relationship with his mother was significant, but I remained unclear as to how it fit into the picture.

I was sure that this last session would create a break-through. Instead, it only sprang slight leaks in which I was given bits and pieces about his childhood and his relation-ship with his parents.

His parents had been very young when they married. His mother became pregnant with Mitch shortly after marrying. They had no money so his father enlisted in the Navy. It was here that he learned electronics and ended up being stationed aboard a submarine, causing him to be away from home for long stretches of time. He remained in the Navy until Mitch was about five years old. Once back in civilian life, he used his electronics background to secure a good job in the aerospace industry.

His mother aspired to being a mom. She loved it and, according to Mitch, never complained like other moms. She tried to have other children, finally giving up after eight years. Just after she had accepted that she would have no more children, she became pregnant with Mitch's sister. She fussed like crazy over the new baby yet always man-aged to find time to devote to Mitch.

Mitch described his parents as "perfect for each other." He could never remember them fighting. His mother loved to do things for the family and was very anxious to please. There was a lot of affection in his family—too much as far as Mitch was concerned. His mom and dad were always kissing each other and, like most kids, Mitch found it em-barrassing.

On the surface, Mitch's family life certainly didn't fit my expected picture. Mitch described a loving, accepting home, not a home filled with the kind of rejection that leads to social phobia and the need to retreat to a fantasy world. There was an inconsistency here somewhere. In thinking it through, I kept coming back to the question of why Mitch would feel anger toward a woman he described as loving.

In our sessions, I kept trying to get an answer to this question. Even though Mitch was not nearly as closed off as when we first met, he still wasn't giving me much to go on. He couldn't remember any reason why he'd be angry with his mother. "Mom's okay," he'd say. "She just smothers me too much. That's all." The curiosity he expressed that one day was now gone. Mitch had again walled up any emotions around this issue and was not yet willing to let me back in.

Mitch had been in therapy with me for a little more than a year, and, although I knew more about him, I still felt he was holding back a lot. I realized that he had managed to mold the sessions to fit his coping style; they had taken on the sameness and predictability that was so characteristic of the rest of his life. Our talks always ended up going in circles. His one-dimensional thinking hampered any attempts at progress. I would probe deeper; he would cling to the surface and, when pushed, would retreat to fantasy.

"Mitch, you'll never be able to have sex with a woman if you don't deal with your fear of rejection."

"I'm not afraid of rejection. I just want to get laid."

"How do you expect that to happen without risking rejection?"

"It happens to other guys and they don't have to ask."

"That's pure fantasy, Mitch. All guys who have had sex with a woman have stuck their necks out by making some sort of overtures."

"What about that guy I know at work?" And with this response we would be back at the starting point.

Nothing was changing and yet Mitch attended his sessions religiously. Why, I wondered? Then it occurred to me that he had entered therapy because he felt pressure from his peers. The step toward therapy, however, seemed to have relieved the pressure to do anything about his life. It must be because therapy was now serving the same purpose as his movies: a way to avoid dealing with the real world. He had become addicted to the sessions just as he was addicted to his movies. He could go to therapy and believe he was doing something to change his life. The reality was that, unknowingly, Mitch had turned the problem of his virginity over to me.

This abdicating of responsibility is a common occurrence in therapy. It's a form of wishful and childlike thinking. The therapist becomes a shaman of sorts who will somehow magically make the person's life more fulfilling without his having to face his fears or pain. Of course, it's a setup for the therapist who eventually will be blamed when nothing changes in the patient's life. The therapist is not a magician, and change doesn't occur until the patient confronts his or her fears and stops being afraid.

Mitch's retreat into fantasy was an excellent defense against facing his fears and one that I had failed to penetrate. Even though Mitch did a great deal to hide it, I knew our relationship meant a lot to him. I was the only real person beside his parents that he had any contact with. But he was unintentionally using this connection as a way to avoid dealing with reality. Because our relationship was the only leverage I had, I decided to use it in an attempt to introduce some anxiety, hoping that the anxiety would motivate him to confront his fears. In the beginning of our next session I said, "Do you think I'm helping you much, Mitch?"

I could tell he immediately sensed that this was a new tactic. His eyes actually flashed at me for a moment, and he fidgeted in his chair. "Well, I haven't gotten laid, if that's what you mean."

"That's true. The therapy hasn't changed that, has it?" He was silent. I remained silent. I wanted him to determine the next step.

Finally, in a rather defiant tone, he asked, "Are you going to kick me out?"

"What makes you think I would kick you out?"

"Isn't that what you were telling me? That you didn't want me around anymore?"

"No, Mitch. Why would you assume that? Have you felt that before? That someone didn't want you around?"

Suddenly, Mitch was standing up and heading for the door. "Forget it," he said. "You don't give a damn about me." He slammed the door on his way out.

Now I was more convinced than ever that somewhere along the way Mitch had been "kicked out" of someone's life and left with the feeling that he wasn't wanted anymore. Given his fear of women, this someone was most likely a woman, probably his mother, but perhaps someone else that Mitch either wasn't talking about or had repressed. I had gambled that by activating his fear, we might make some progress. I'd have to wait to see if he came back to know if my gamble had paid off.

As it turned out, I didn't hear from Mitch at all. He didn't call and didn't show up for his next appointment or any after that. I thought about him often over the following months, wondering if I had made a mistake in trying to use his vulnerability to force the issue. Had I prematurely pushed him to face his fear, thus breaking the only real connection he had in his life?

My answer to that question came in an unexpected way. One evening as I left my office, I encountered a man leaning up against the hallway wall opposite my door. I felt a surge of adrenaline as I took in the fact that a strange man seemed to be loitering. Then he called my name and I felt brave enough to take a closer look. I was taken aback when I realized it was Mitch. He didn't look anything like the Mitch I knew from before. His hair was longer and more stylish, and he had on tight-fitting jeans, a plaid shirt, and a pair of loafers. All of this adorned a slimmer, firmer body.

The black-framed glasses were gone; in their place was a pair of rimless, lightly tinted, fashionable glasses.

"Hi. Mind if I walk with you to your car?" he asked.

"Sure. I didn't recognize you at first. You look different," I said.

"Yeah, I know. Everyone at work says the same thing."

"I've thought about you often, Mitch. I knew I was taking a risk at our last session by challenging you. I assumed I lost because I seemed to have lost you. Did I?"

"I was pissed, all right. But a lot has happened since then."

"It appears it has."

"Can I come back to see you? I think I'm ready to work this time."

My curiosity was certainly piqued. Was this the same guy? He looked different from the Mitch I knew and talked differently, too. I was eager to know what had happened in the last six months. "Of course you can come back, Mitch. I never wanted you to leave in the first place."

"You didn't?"

"No. If I remember correctly, you jumped to that conclusion on your own."

"So, can I have my same appointment time back?" he asked.

I smiled to myself as I realized he hadn't changed all that much. "The only evening appointment I have open is on a different day. Is that going to be a problem?"

He hesitated for a moment. I could tell he was struggling with some internal process. Finally, he said, "Okay. Tell me what day and I'll be there."

In the sessions that followed, Mitch told me what had been happening in his life in the last months. It was a fascinating story. What made it even more remarkable was that it was true, not a creation of his fantasy world.

When he left my office he had been furious. He had stopped at the video store on his way home and picked up his usual movies. But for the first time, he did not get aroused. Instead, he felt bored and restless. They didn't take him away into another world as they usually did. Impulsively, he got in his car and found himself driving to a striptease bar near his office. He had driven past the bar hundreds of times and had often thought he would stop in, but he never had.

He parked the car, but instead of going in, he sat in the car for a long time. He thought about what it would be like inside. There would be people he didn't know, and they would think him foolish, maybe even laugh at him. Finally, he decided he'd just go back home. It was safer at home; at home he had to face only himself. He started the car and drove about a block before he heard a voice inside his head saying, "How do you expect your life to change if you stay home all the time? You've got to take some risks if you want your life to be different." He knew it was my voice and he remembered thinking, "I'll show her I can take a risk." He drove around the block and turned into the parking lot of the bar. This time he didn't give himself a chance to think about backing out. Once inside, he was surprised to find he felt as if the place and the people were familiar. In the movies he had seen many such faces and places.

At first he didn't realize that he was slipping into a role, acting as if he was following a script. He just knew that he felt fearless and arrogant like all the macho movie studs he had seen operating hundreds of times. He sat down casually at a table, not in the least self-conscious that he was alone. When the waitress asked for his drink order, he found himself looking her directly in the eyes as he ordered. Then he focused his attention on the blonde, bare-chested female undulating on the stage to music. He remembered thinking how beautiful she was and how much she looked like the women he had seen in his movies.

Suddenly, this goddess of a woman was walking off the

stage and moving toward the audience. She stood in front of a man seated at a table across the room, brushing her large breasts across his face, all the time rotating her scantily clad pelvis in circles. Mitch was transfixed by what he saw and could feel himself getting hard; this was an erection unlike any he'd ever had before. Then the woman moved away from that man and started walking toward his side of the room. The feelings of arrogance and self-confidence vanished, leaving panic in their place. What if she comes over to me, he thought? The next thing he knew she was sitting on his lap, her legs straddling him and her large breasts touching his chest. His heart was pounding so much he thought that surely she could feel the pulsations in her breasts. She ran her fingers through his hair and leaned over as if to kiss him but instead whispered in his ear, "Keep it hard for me, baby. I'll be back." Then she stood up and walked back to the stage. The music stopped and she disappeared into the black shadows of the side curtains.

Mitch looked around the room to see if anybody was watching him, but no one seemed to notice or care that he felt as if his body would explode. Another woman was on the stage now, but Mitch didn't think her nearly as beautiful. He could still smell the aroma of the blonde who moments before had been in his lap. Mitch kept reassuring himself that she was real and that he wasn't dreaming or watching a movie. The waitress came up to him to ask him if he wanted another drink. He couldn't get any words out so he just nodded yes. He remained, nursing his drink for a long time, hoping the blonde would perform again.

As time passed and she didn't appear, he began to get anxious. Maybe he'd never see her again, he thought. No, he'd find a way to see her again. He'd have to because he was sure he wouldn't be able to live unless he saw her again. Finally, however, she did come back for a second performance. This time she didn't come into the audience, but Mitch didn't care. He was happy just watching her.

And watch her he did. Now, instead of stopping at the video store, Mitch would get something to eat on his way home from work and then head for the bar. True to his nature, the behavior became habituated, and soon he was considered to be a "regular." People would actually say hello to him when he walked in. This was the first time in his life that anybody "knew" who he was. Mitch began to feel as comfortable in the bar as he did at home. He found out the names of the waitresses and began calling them by name. He also quizzed them about the blonde sex goddess and found out her name was Angel. It fit her perfectly, he thought.

Eventually, Mitch and Angel developed a relationship of sorts. At least in Mitch's mind it seemed like a relationship. When Angel was on the stage, she would wink at him and do a few bump and grinds in his direction. Sometimes she would come down into the audience and sit in his lap or shimmy her breasts in front of him. Mitch took these behaviors as signs that Angel thought he was special—not just another dude out for his sexual fix.

Returning home at night after her performance, he would masturbate to fantasies of himself with Angel and then drift off into a pleasant sleep. Sometimes he would dream of her. The dreams all had themes of Angel reaching out to him and drawing him in, gently holding him to her breasts while he rested safe and secure in her embrace. The weeks passed and Mitch became obsessed with thoughts of being with Angel. How could he approach her? What would he say if he did? Could he tell her how he felt? But then his thoughts would be interrupted by fear. What if she didn't want him? This last thought so tormented him that he would force it out of his mind, preferring instead to imagine himself embraced by her.

In his mind, he played with several different ways he might get her to notice him. Finally, he decided he would send her some flowers. He couldn't go wrong if he did that. In the movies, all the women liked flowers. Certainly she wouldn't turn down the flowers, and maybe she'd even come over to his table after the show. He had never sent flowers before and wasn't sure how it was done, so he stopped at a flower shop one evening before going to the bar. When he walked in, he immediately noticed he was alone in the shop except for a young girl behind the counter. He was momentarily frozen when he realized he would have to talk to this girl if he wanted to get the flowers. Surely she would notice he had never done this before and think him foolish. His first impulse was to leave. But if he walked out now, he might never get to be with Angel. So, without looking the girl in the eyes, he mumbled, "I want to send some flowers to my girlfriend." He watched out of the corner of his eye to see if the girl was laughing at him, but she simply smiled and asked, "What kind of flowers would you like to send?"

Her question surprised him. He hadn't gotten that far in his thinking. How stupid of me, he thought. He said the first thing that came into his mind: "Roses, I guess."

"Roses are nice. What color would you like?" she asked.

"Color?" He hadn't counted on having to decide that either. He thought all roses were red. He'd be safe if he said that. "Red. Yeah, I'd like red," he said with a little more conviction.

"Do you want a dozen?"

"Yeah, a dozen," he said. He remembered from somewhere that a dozen roses sounded familiar.

"Why don't you write out the card while I get them ready," she replied.

Mitch felt his body flush with heat as her words sunk in. He'd have to write a card. When he had thought of sending flowers, it hadn't occurred to him that he'd have to enclose a card. The girl handed him a pen and a card and then left to go into another room toward the back of the store. When he looked at the card, he noticed it had a red rose in one corner. Somehow, just seeing this made him feel that his choice was probably okay.

He stood for a long time with the pen and card in his hand, not knowing what to do. Should he just sign his name? Maybe he should he tell her how beautiful he thought she was? He was sure the girl in the shop would return and notice he didn't know what to do and think he was a fool. The longer he stood there immobilized, the more undecided he felt about how to sign the card. The girl came back into the room and Mitch knew he couldn't stall any longer. So, he quickly wrote, *From an admirer,* then handed the card to the girl. He watched as she put the card inside the long-handled plastic forklike thing that was with the flowers.

"Are you paying by cash or credit card?" she asked.

My God, he thought. I didn't even think about paying. He never used credit cards and wasn't sure exactly how much cash he had on him. "Uh . . . cash, I guess. He could feel his heart beating as he heard himself ask, "How much are they?" Please let me have enough money, he thought.

"With tax it comes to fifty-five dollars."

Mitch felt a pain deep in his stomach. He had no idea that it would cost so much. But it was too late now. If he didn't have the money, then the girl would know for sure what a fool he was. He pulled out his wallet and hesitantly looked inside. He could feel a rush of relief as he saw three twenties plus some ones. He paid the girl, waited for his change, and then started to leave.

"Sir," she called after him. "You forgot your flowers."

"Aren't you going to deliver them?" he answered in surprise.

"Well, we can, of course. But it will cost more and we need the address."

Mitch just stood there. Again, he didn't know what to do. He didn't have enough money, and besides, he would never be able to tell this girl where he wanted the flowers sent. For a second he wished he had never started the whole mess. Finally he said, "No, I'll just take them." She handed him the roses, and as he took them, he felt a sharp pain that caused him to wince and cry out.

"Be careful of the thorns," the girl said.

"Yeah, sure. I forgot," Mitch replied. As he walked out the door, he felt a tremendous sense of relief. He was very glad this part was over. He felt sure the girl knew he was a jerk but consoled himself with the thought that he would never have to see her again and that if there was a next time, he'd know what to expect.

Once in his car and driving over to the bar, the relief he felt upon leaving the store was replaced by apprehension about how he would get the flowers to Angel and about how he had signed the card. He would look stupid walking into the bar with flowers, and besides, he didn't want anyone to know he was giving them to her. And if he just left them at her door she wouldn't know who sent them. Then an even worse thought entered his head: Maybe men sent her flowers all the time. He would really feel foolish if this was the case. He didn't want to be one of many admirers. The thought of other men in her life caused a sharp, burning pain in his chest. It was a pain so deep and dark that he felt it was literally splitting him apart. Then he felt blackness completely surround him as if every bit of light in the world had been suddenly turned out.

The next thing he knew he heard a horn blasting at him. He looked in the rearview mirror and saw a line of cars behind him. He looked up at the traffic light and saw that it was green. How long had he been sitting there? he wondered. He stepped on the gas and as soon as possible turned into a side street and pulled over to the curb. He felt a little confused. Where had he been headed? Had he blacked out? Then he noticed the flowers on the seat next to him, and he remembered he had been on his way to the bar to see Angel. The next thing he remembered was the pain he had felt. He couldn't recall what brought it on, but it must have caused him to black out.

He drove over to the bar, sitting inside his car for a long

time, trying to decide what to do with the flowers. What would they do in the movies? he thought. Then it came to him. He'd give a kid a few bucks to deliver them. He picked up the flowers, got out of his car, and walked over to the street. It was a pretty busy street, but he didn't see any kids hanging around. He waited for what seemed like half an hour, but nobody came walking by. He was about to give up when a pickup truck stopped at the intersection where he was standing. There were a few teenage kids in the back of the truck and he yelled at them, "Hey, you wanna make a few bucks?" But the truck took off, leaving the kids staring at him. He stood there feeling dumb. What was he going to do now? He couldn't stand there all night asking strangers if they wanted to make some money. He was about to leave when the pickup truck pulled over to the curb in front of him.

"What d'you got in mind, mister?" one of the kids asked.

Mitch was paralyzed. Again, he was caught feeling naive—of not thinking far enough ahead. He knew it was too late to back out. Pointing in the direction of the bar, he said, "I'll give you a few bucks if you'll deliver these flowers to the bar over there."

"How many bucks?" one of the kids asked.

It was then that Mitch remembered he didn't have much money left. He knew he had at least five ones but didn't have any idea if that would be enough. He'd have to take a chance. "Five," he said.

"Okay, mister," one kid said and then vaulted over the side of the truck and walked over to Mitch. "Who should I give them to?"

"When you go inside, ask for Nick. Don't give them to anybody else. Tell Nick they're for Angel. You got that? For Angel."

"Yeah, I got it. Where's the money?"

Mitch handed the flowers to the kid so he could get his wallet out. He could feel his hands shaking. What if he got mugged? Or what if the kid ran off with his money and the flowers? At the same time he was thinking this, he was handing the kid the money, then he was relieved to see him run the fifty yards to the bar and disappear inside. In what seemed like less than a minute, Mitch saw him come out the front door and run toward him. He didn't bother to stop. "No problem, man," the kid said as he ran past him and once again vaulted himself into the back of the truck. He pounded on the glass behind the driver and the truck burned rubber as it took off.

As he watched the truck speed off, Mitch felt a tremendous sense of relief. He hadn't been mugged after all, and the flowers had been delivered. As he slowly walked back to his car he felt something he'd never felt before—an exhilaration at having overcome obstacles. He even thought to himself that maybe what I had said to him over and over again was true: It feels powerful to confront your fears.

The good feelings didn't last long. When he got back to his car, he didn't know whether to go inside the bar or go home. He had only a few dollars left, not even enough to buy a drink. And anyway, he hadn't signed the card so Angel wouldn't know who sent them. He started to feel stupid again. All that effort and she wouldn't know who sent them. All he could think of was what a jerk he was. He started feeling terribly depressed and decided he'd just go home. As he drove back to his apartment, the feelings of depression intensified. He was stupid to think flowers would get her attention. For the first time, he thought maybe it was good he hadn't signed the card. She wouldn't know what a fool he was.

The depression stayed with him for days. He had trouble concentrating at work and after work would drive by the bar but not go in. He tried going back to the video stores and renting his movies, but even that didn't lift the depression. He couldn't concentrate on the movies either. They didn't give him the same warm, arousing feelings he used to get watching them. And besides, seeing the women in the movies only made him miss Angel even more.

After four days of not going to the bar, Mitch was beside himself. He would pace his apartment at night when he couldn't sleep. Finally, he decided he couldn't stay away any longer. He stopped in the bar on a Friday night—exactly a week since he had had the kid drop off the flowers. When he walked in, a few regulars called out to him, asking him where he'd been. One guy even said he had missed him. Mitch felt great. Nobody had ever noticed what he did, and certainly nobody had ever missed him.

Then he noticed that somebody was sitting at his favorite table. At first, Mitch didn't know what to do. He always sat at that table. He just knew it wouldn't be the same at another table. He stood there for a few moments trying to decide what to do and finally took a seat close by. After a while, he realized that it felt okay at this table. He was surprised and pleased at this feeling. The depressed feeling of the previous week was completely gone. And when Angel came on the stage, he felt the old excitement return. It was great just watching her. Maybe he didn't need to meet her after all, he thought. It was enough just to watch her. He was feeling good tonight. He wouldn't spoil it with thoughts of finding ways to meet her.

She left the stage and another woman he had seen many times took her place. He watched her carefully, comparing her to Angel. She's okay, but she's not gorgeous like Angel, he thought. He was so engrossed in his comparison that he didn't notice at first that someone was sitting down at his table. When he finally looked around, he was startled. Angel was sitting across from him, her body covered by a loose-fitting, multicolored silk robe.

"Hello," she said.

Mitch was speechless. He wanted to say something, anything, but he couldn't even say hello.

"It was you that sent the flowers, wasn't it? I wouldn't have guessed, but you didn't show up for a week afterward, so I figured it must be you. Am I right?"

Still, Mitch couldn't find any words. Then Angel reached

out, put her hand on top of his, and said, "It's okay. I loved them. They were beautiful."

Her hand felt warm and soft, and he was again flooded with the same feeling he had when Janet had shook his hand. It was a reassuring feeling and yet it made him anxious. He stared at Angel. If she hadn't touched his hand, he might have thought he was imagining her there—a vision of his own creation. He knew he must say something. Otherwise she might leave. The next thing he knew he was saying, "You're so beautiful. I love watching you." Mitch didn't even believe it was him talking. Where did he get the courage to say those words when he could hardly even talk?

"You're a sweetie to say that. What's your name?"

"Mitch."

"I like that name. It has a masculine sound to it."

Not once in his life had Mitch ever thought his name sounded masculine, and yet, here was this goddess of beauty telling him his name sounded masculine.

"Thanks. I like your name too. I come here just to see you. The other girls don't compare to you."

"Well, aren't you a honey to say such nice things. You going to stick around until my next performance?"

"I always do."

"How about you and I go for a cup of coffee after the show?"

Was this possible? Was Angel really asking him to go for coffee? Maybe he was dreaming? He moved his hand just a bit to see if he could still feel her hand on his. Yes, her hand was really there.

"Sure," was all he could say.

"Well, you just stay right here. I'll come out and get you when I'm finished and I'm dressed."

Mitch could hardly contain himself. How could he wait without going crazy? He didn't want to drink too much because he might do something really stupid. But he was so nervous, and that meant he was sure to do something foolish anyway. He'd just have a few more drinks, but not so many that he would get drunk. He didn't want Angel to see him drunk.

The wait seemed like an eternity. Then a really fearful thought entered his head. What if she didn't show up? Why was she being nice to him anyway? Maybe she was pulling a joke on him. All of these fears ran around in his head, and by the time Angel had finished her second performance, his nerves were raw. The couple of drinks didn't seem to help. He sat transfixed in his chair, not knowing what else to do. It seemed like he waited a very long time after she left the stage. Now his fears of her not showing were mounting. Then, suddenly, someone was sitting at his table, but it didn't look like Angel.

"Sorry, honey. It takes a while to get all the junky makeup off," the person said.

Mitch was staring at the woman sitting across from him. She looked older and plainer without all the makeup, and her hair wasn't really blonde. It was more brown, and now it was pulled back and tied at the neck rather than swirling like a mane around her face. She was wearing jeans and a sweatshirt, and she no longer looked like the girls in the movies. Mitch was puzzled. Could this be the same person? he wondered. Angel must have read his thoughts because she said, "Guess I look different without all the stage props, huh?"

"I thought you had blonde hair," Mitch heard himself saying.

"No, that's a wig. I wear it for the show. Men like blondes," she said with a twinge of hostility. "Look, you want to forget about going out for coffee now that you've seen the real me?"

"No. NO! I just didn't realize how much makeup changes things."

"Yeah, I know. That's why I wear it . . . . So, I'd like to get out of here. You ready?"

"Yeah, sure. I'm ready."

They went to an all-night coffee shop and talked. Well, Angel talked while Mitch listened. He was glad she did all the talking because that way he wouldn't say something stupid. Still, the entire time Mitch felt fearful that he would somehow blow it and would never see Angel again. But his fears didn't materialize; he and Angel frequently went out for coffee after her performance. Angel liked the fact that Mitch was a good listener. She'd never met a man who was willing to let her talk. Most of the men she had spent time with only wanted one thing: sex. But Mitch was different, she said.

As the weeks passed, Mitch began to relax a bit when he was around Angel. His fear that she would disappear from his life didn't go away completely, but as they spent more and more time together, it didn't preoccupy him nearly as much. He was relieved that she made only momentary complaints that Mitch rarely talked about himself. ''I don't know a thing about you,'' she would say. But if Mitch changed the subject (which he usually did), she'd forget about it and not press him for information. Mostly, she talked about herself. Her two favorite subjects were how she became a striptease dancer and her recent breakup with a boyfriend.

According to Angel, she had never intended to be dancing nude in front of men. Twenty years ago she was Sara, not Angel, and as Sara she had met and married a man who owned a striptease bar. Since her husband spent most of his time at the bar, she began to hang out there as well. It was then that she discovered her husband treated his dancers as if they were a harem. Angel soon learned she was expected to accept his affairs or get out. At twenty she hated her life but felt trapped because she didn't know how she would make a living. She remained married and miserable for five years until one of the dancers befriended her and told her, ''If you can't beat 'em, join 'em.''

Angel hated the dancers; it never occurred to her she

might become one. But as she thought more and more about it, she felt sure she could do what they did. It was no big deal to move your body around to music, and Angel knew she had a great body. She also knew the extent of the makeup and costumes they put on to look the way they did. So with her new friend's connections, she left Sara behind, became Angel, and got herself a job in another bar. There was great satisfaction in keeping this a secret from her husband—but the secret didn't last long. When he found out, he called her a whore and told her to get out. By now, however, she was making pretty good money, and getting out was what she had intended all along. What she didn't intend was for the dancing to become permanent. But here she was at forty, still dancing and still hating her life. This always brought her to her next favorite subject: the jerk who didn't keep his promise of marriage. She said very little about the man himself, only about how she was living with broken dreams.

Mitch didn't mind that Angel sounded like a broken record. The experience of spending time with a woman was so completely different for him that he looked forward to every second they had together. They even began to spend some time together during the day on the weekends. That's when Angel started taking Mitch shopping. She made suggestions about what she thought would look good on him, and Mitch actually found he enjoyed trying on clothes for her and letting her decide what looked best. Then she suggested that he let his hair grow and that he change his glasses. Mitch had never given much thought to his appearance before, but he enjoyed having Angel take an interest in how he looked.

Yet spending time with her was tearing him apart. In his mind, Angel was two different women. One was his plain-looking friend whom he felt increasingly comfortable around. The other was the exotic and sexy topless dancer whom he lusted after and wanted desperately to take to bed. Blending the two together seemed impossible to Mitch; keeping them apart left him feeling lonely and sexually frustrated.

His relationship with the "two" Angels was an emotional roller coaster. When he was with his plain-looking friend, he had very little sexual desire. Angel seemed pleased by this and repeatedly told him how much she appreciated his nonsexual friendship. But when he saw her on the stage, he was filled with desire for her. He felt certain he would lose his friend if he tried to gain a lover. Besides, having sex with her was out of the question because she'd discover that he had never been with a woman and think him terribly retarded and foolish. Once she discovered this she would never see him again. He couldn't stand it if that happened. He would just have to deal with his sexual frustration, he decided.

He thought he had it under control until, about five months into their relationship, Angel told him that she'd received a call from the ex-boyfriend. Angel sought Mitch's advice on whether she should give him another chance. It was only at this point that Angel admitted that he had left her for another women. When Mitch heard this, his first response was to feel a deep pain inside—as if it had happened to him, not her. He was puzzled by this response, but only for a short time, because as Angel continued to talk about how much this man had hurt her, Mitch became angry. The more she talked, the angrier he became. He didn't understand his anger, but he did feel sure that if the man were to come anywhere near him, he would certainly kill him. Of course, he didn't tell Angel any of this. Instead, he just listened. But as the days went on and she continued to stew over whether to see him again, Mitch could no longer contain his anger. After about her tenth time of lamenting about not knowing what to do, he blurted out, "If I ever see that son of a bitch, I'll kill him." Angel was startled by his reaction. Mitch had always been a shoulder to cry on, not explosive and reactive.

"What brought that on?" she asked.

"How can you even consider seeing him again? He's already dumped you once. Isn't that enough?"

Angel snapped back at him, "I told you. He says he now realizes he made a mistake. He wants me back."

"You're crazy if you take him back. He'll dump you again."

"How can you be so sure? You don't even know him."

"I don't have to know him. You can't trust someone who's kicked you out. I know that for sure."

"You do, huh? What makes you such an expert?" she hurled back at him.

Suddenly, he stood up from the table where they had been seated, knocking his chair over in the process. "You don't give a damn about me. All you can think about is yourself. Well, I'm sick of it. Go back to him. Get your heart broken again. See if I care." Then he stormed out of the restaurant with everyone staring after him, especially Angel.

Mitch drove recklessly back to his apartment. He knew he was risking his life the way he was driving, but he didn't care. He wasn't so sure he wanted to live. He couldn't remember ever being so angry. Once inside his apartment, he paced up and down his living room, repeatedly telling himself that neither one of his two Angels really cared about him. In fact, the truth was, no one cared about him. At this thought, he walked over to a *Playboy* centerfold on his wall. As he stared at it, transfixed by the image, he thought he saw Angel's face staring back at him. He ripped the picture from the wall, tearing it into shreds and scattering the pieces around the room. As he did this, he felt the anger begin to diminish, leaving him with another, equally miserable, feeling. It wasn't a completely new feeling, but he had never felt it so strongly before. He wasn't sure, but he thought it was depression. This feeling that Mitch thought must be depression caused him to do something he had rarely done in his life—ask questions.

Why was this happening to him? He hadn't intended to fight with Angel; she meant so much to him. He tried to figure out what had come over him. He kept replaying the scene in his mind, trying to understand why he had reacted so strongly. The strong reaction seemed so familiar to him. He racked his brain to recall when he had last felt this exact same feeling but came up with no answers, only more questions.

The feelings of despair intensified and prevented him from sleeping. Lying in bed unable to sleep, he thought about his videos. Ever since going to the bar he had not rented any videos. But he remembered that they always helped him get to sleep before. He got up, put on his clothes, and drove to the closest video store, renting one of his favorite movies. He hoped watching it would make the bad feelings go away.

But he couldn't concentrate on the movie. Instead, his mind kept flipping around from one thought to another as if searching through a Rolodex looking for the right card. He felt sure he was losing his mind. This made him think about needing some help, which made him think about therapy. He hadn't thought about therapy since the day he walked out of my office. It was then that the realization hit him. The familiar feeling he was trying to place earlier now revealed itself. It was the exact feeling he experienced when he was last in my my office. The Rolodex of his mind finally settled on the right card as he realized he had yelled out exactly the same words to Angel as he had yelled to me: "You don't give a damn about me."

Was it true? he asked himself. Did the only two women he had ever connected with really not give a damn? Or was he reacting to something else? He remembered what I had told him often enough: that his fear of rejection from women was deep-rooted and would continue to haunt him until he confronted this fear. Was I right? Would he find rejection where it didn't exist? And if so, why?

And what had gotten into him that he was asking himself

all these questions? He wasn't used to asking questions about himself. Why was he doing it now? And why couldn't he stop asking all these questions? He felt like someone was showing him flash cards, and a new card with a new question was in front of him before he could think about an answer to the previous question.

Then a whole new chain of questions ran through his mind. Why had he gone to see a therapist in the first place? Before coming to see me he had been fairly content. He only wanted to have sex with a woman, not deal with why he hadn't had sex. Before therapy his life had been predictable and comfortable. He never felt despair or depression the way he was feeling it now. Perhaps it was a mistake to have seen a therapist. But if he hadn't gone to therapy he would never have been so mad at me and he never would have met Angel. If he hadn't taken a risk by going to the bar, she would never have entered his life. Of course, then he wouldn't be feeling this despair. Was meeting her worth it?

He felt so confused. Should he go back to therapy? Or should he just try to forget Angel and go back to his life the way it was before any of this happened? Could he go back in time? he wondered. This was the last thought he had as he finally drifted off into a restless sleep, soon followed by a terrifying dream.

In his dream he was in a hallway with lots of doors. The doors were tall, ten feet at least, and he could barely reach the handles. Inside the hallway he could sense that there was danger, and he knew that on the other side of the doors lay safety. He was running from door to door trying to open them, but they must have been locked because he couldn't open any of them. He shoved and pushed, trying to get the doors open, but they wouldn't budge. With each door he couldn't open, he felt the danger increase, and he tried even harder to open a door, any door. As he failed again and again in his attempts, he felt the danger in the hallway increase along with a panicky feeling inside him. Then he heard a loud warning alarm going off, and he knew impending doom was close by. Then another warning alarm. Suddenly he was awake, his heart pounding and his breathing rapid. He was no longer in the hallway. Instead he was in his bedroom. He looked around his room, trying to get his bearings. He breathed a sigh of relief as he realized he had been dreaming.

Just as he was losing some of the panicky feeling, he was startled by the same warning alarm he had heard in his dream. He lay there for a moment, feeling drugged and unable to clear his head. The warning alarm sounded again, and it was then that he realized the sound was coming from his telephone. Mitch had so rarely heard his telephone ring that at first he hadn't recognized the sound. He picked up the receiver and mumbled a weak hello.

It was his boss on the phone. As soon as Mitch heard his voice, he glanced at the clock radio. It was after 10:00 A.M. He bolted out of bed, not sure what move to make next. He had never slept through his radio alarm before. In fact, he'd never even been late to work in the twelve years he'd been with the company. Not even with all the late hours he'd been keeping since meeting Angel.

"Mitch, is that you?" he heard his boss saying.

"Yeah."

"Are you okay? We got worried down here. You've never missed a day with us. I thought I'd call. Are you all right?"

"Uh . . . Maybe I got something . . . you know . . . like the flu or something."

"Well, you stay home today. You deserve a day off. I was just calling to see if you're all right. Now that I've talked to you and know you're okay . . . well, I just want you to take care of yourself. Call me later if you think you want to stay home tomorrow as well."

"No, I'll be in tomorrow for sure."

"Just take it easy. Feel better, okay?"

"Yeah. Okay. Bye."

After he hung up, he sat down on the bed trying to remember the dream he'd had. It had been a frightening dream, but now he couldn't remember much about it. But he did remember the argument he'd had with Angel and immediately felt anxious. The anxiety was increased by the thought of what he would do with his day. He wasn't used to having an unstructured day, and he felt very uneasy about it. He liked it so much better when he knew ahead of time exactly what he would be doing. Well, whenever he had free time he worked on his software program, he thought. So, he'd do that. He got dressed and had what he always had for breakfast: instant coffee and a bowl of cereal. Then he sat down at his computer to work.

He stared at the screen for a long time. His mind didn't seem to want to focus on the screen. Instead, the same thoughts and questions of last night kept doing a war dance in his head. Why did he blow up? He knew there was some relationship to his last therapy sessions and the previous night with Angel. Should he go back to therapy? Or should he just try and forget Angel and go back to his previous life? Eventually, he turned off his computer, realizing he wouldn't be able to get anything done.

For the first time he could ever remember, he felt lonely. He hated the feeling and didn't want to be alone in his apartment with his thoughts. But the only person other than his parents he'd ever spent time with was Angel. Maybe he would drive over to her place and see what she was doing, he thought. He looked at his watch. It was only 11:30. Perhaps she'd want to go to lunch.

Angel seemed surprised to see him at her door. She was dressed up, wearing makeup and her blonde wig. Seeing her this way unsettled Mitch. She never wore heavy makeup or the wig when she was with him. As he stood in the doorway looking at her, he could feel the familiar beginnings of sexual arousal. He felt himself flush with embarrassment, but that didn't seem to stop his body from reacting. The fantasy of being in bed with Angel flashed in his mind and he was aware of a growing excitement within him—an excitement that seemed to have a momentum and power separate from his rational mind. If Angel hadn't spoken—said what she said—Mitch might have lost control. But, unknowingly, she broke the spell with her words.

"Look, Mitch. I don't know what got into you last night. I thought you were my friend. Instead, you go acting like some kind of jerk, trying to tell me what I can and can't do. Roger is coming over here any minute and we're going to lunch. I decided to see him again."

Mitch felt as if he had been punched in the stomach. The mounting sexual desire vanished, extinguished like a fire that was suddenly deprived of its source of fuel. Now, instead of desire, he felt anger—the same anger he had felt last night.

"How come you're dressed like that?" he heard himself say. "You never dress like that for me."

"Roger likes me this way, that's why. And besides, it's none of your business how I dress with other men."

The last two words devastated Mitch. The punch he had felt in his stomach now felt like a fist in his face. Angel must have sensed she had gone too far because she said, "Look, Mitch, I'm sorry. But I've decided to see Roger and it really isn't your business who I go out with. We'll go out for coffee after the show tonight and we'll talk about it. But right now you better go. Roger won't like it if he finds you here. He won't understand our friendship. Please go." Then she closed the door on him.

Mitch returned to his car, sitting inside and trying to cope with the emotions he was feeling. Then he saw a man pull up, get out of his car, and go to Angel's door. He watched as she let him inside. He could feel a pain deep within him, as if someone had just poisoned him. He decided against waiting any longer. He didn't want to know if they were really going out to lunch or if they would stay inside her place and do something else. An image of Angel in bed with someone else started to enter his mind. It was accompanied by a pain so sharp he thought he might explode.

Then he felt the same blackness as before surround him and with it the vanishing of the pain. He "awoke" to find himself slumped over the steering wheel of his car. At first he didn't know where he was, but slowly the memory of Roger going into Angel's apartment returned. He knew he had to get out of there before he did something dangerous.

He started his car and headed back toward his apartment, once again not caring if he caused an accident. For a minute he played with the fantasy of being killed in a crash and seeing Angel agonizing over his death. He drove on, knowing it wasn't safe for him to be driving, but not caring.

Once inside his apartment, he began to be aware of feeling totally lost—not knowing what to do. He wished he had been killed rather than having to deal with what he was feeling. He lay down on his bed, thinking of ways he might kill himself and wondering if he had the nerve to do it. Finally, around 6:00 P.M., he fell asleep, only to dream again about being in the menacing hallway filled with doors he couldn't open. He woke the next morning at 4:00 A.M., this time the dream still fresh in his mind. He kept going over and over the dream, wondering what it meant. He was feeling anxious and depressed but forced himself to go to work anyway. Being at work was certainly better than facing another day without anything to do. That evening he was standing outside my door waiting for me.

Mitch seemed a very different person from the one I had known months before. In talking about all the things that had happened in his life, he seemed curious, even introspective. For the first time Mitch was asking questions of himself, not just demanding an end to his virginal state. Obviously, the recent events in his life had forced him to confront certain issues previously he had denied. His ritualistic, isolated lifestyle had maintained the denial by controlling what came into his life. Nothing had challenged his denial. By letting Angel into his life, however, he lost that control and along with it the ability to use denial to avoid painful issues.

Now that he was feeling pain, he was motivated to deal with these issues. He now knew that if he didn't deal with his fears, he would never change. Our sessions no longer went in circles, with him retreating into his fantasy world as a way to avoid the pain. Instead he asked question after question.

"Why did I get so angry in that session where I thought you wanted to kick me out? It's the same feeling I had when Angel started talking about Roger."

"You're very vulnerable to the feeling of being kicked out."

"What do you mean 'vulnerable'?"

"It's a tender point with you. Like a bruise that hasn't healed. When somebody touches it, it hurts. As I said to you before, I think in your early childhood you experienced something that caused you to feel kicked out."

"But I don't remember anything like that happening. Except for that time I got sent away to camp. Is it possible that one experience could create this vulnerability you're talking about?"

"It's possible, but not likely. I believe you were already sensitized by that time."

"Sensitized?"

"The more you experience something unpleasant, the more you become sensitive to it. It's like being poked in the arm. Someone can be poking you—not necessarily very hard—but if they keep doing it, you eventually develop a tender bruise. The area remains tender, and when someone touches the sensitive spot, it's very painful. You've been protecting your tender spot by keeping people out of your life."

"So, what I'm sensitive to is being locked out?"

"What did you say?"

"I said, I'm afraid of being kicked out."

134

"No, I'm sure you said *locked* out, not kicked out."

We both looked at each other and knew we were thinking the same thing at the same time. He spoke first. "The dream. In the dream I was locked out."

"Yes, and in the dream the doors were tall. You could hardly reach the handles. To a child a door looks very tall, and a child can hardly reach the handles. Think back, Mitch. Can you ever remember being locked out and feeling something bad would happen to you?"

Mitch remained silent for a moment and finally shook his head no. "I can't remember anything like that," he said.

"Would you be willing to ask your mom about it?"

"Why? What's she got to do with it?"

"I'm not sure. It's just that the sensitivity you have is centered around your fears of being rejected by women. She might be able to recall something you can't."

"What exactly am I supposed to ask her?"

"Ask her if she ever remembers you being really upset by a locked door."

As it turned out, Mitch was very surprised by what his mother had to say. She had answered easily and without hesitation that she certainly did remember because it had been upsetting for her at the time. She said that when Mitch was an infant and up until he was three or four years old, he used to sleep with her whenever his father was deployed on a Navy ship. When his father came back from sea, Mitch would go back into his crib in another room for the few weeks his father was home. During this time, Mitch would wake up crying at night. She would always go to him and rock him until he fell asleep, but he would only wake up later and start crying again. When his father left for another deployment, she would bring him back into her room to stop his crying so she could get some sleep.

His mother told him it got a lot worse when he was old

enough to climb out of his crib. Then, during the times his father was home, he would climb out of the crib, toddle down the hallway, slip into her room, and climb into bed with them. She would get up and take Mitch back to his room. She'd stay with him until he fell asleep, but the scene would be repeated several times each night. Once his father was gone, Mitch would go back to sleeping with his mother. She remembered well a very ugly fight between her and his father when Mitch was around three-and-a-half years old. His father thought he was too old to be sleeping with her when he was away and insisted it had to stop. On that visit home, he had a lock put on Mitch's bedroom door. When he awoke, Mitch would try to get out of his room. Unable to open the door, he would stand at the door crying for what seemed like an eternity. His mother wanted to go to him, but his father insisted that Mitch would have to cry it out—it was the only way he would break the habit. Finally, he would cry himself to sleep on the floor in front of his door. After more than a week of this, he began to sleep through the entire night in his own bed.

After listening to Mitch repeat his mother's story, the way he lived his life made much more sense to me. Being kicked out and then locked out from his place of security was the fear that dictated Mitch's life. As a child, there was love, comfort, and security sleeping with his mother—that is, until another man, a stranger, came into her life. Then Mitch was *rejected* in favor of him. Eventually, this man would cease to be a stranger, but by then it was too late to undo the damage. Unknowingly to all involved, these episodes created a permanently tender place in the structure of Mitch's personality.

Then in grade school the episode with the neighborhood girl happened, further bruising this structure and, coincidentally, associating sexuality with rejection. When this incident happened, Mitch unconsciously promised himself he would never expose his tender place again. He kept his promise to himself by closing ranks. He built a wall of insulation around his tender place by ritualizing his life, downplaying his physical attributes, and shying away from girls. Instead, he directed his energy to an area with no personal involvement and where he would receive no rejection: computer technology.

Mitch's defensive scheme was successful in keeping further rejection out of his life. However, his unconscious plan didn't work as well on his developing sexuality. Trying to sweep powerful sexual urges under the rug most often results in their reappearance in a distorted manner at the other end. In Mitch's case, to satisfy these urges, he discovered, like many other men, that pornography allowed sexual expression without the risk of rejection. With pornography, one simply turns on by turning a page or turning on a screen. In the fantasy world of pornography, men can have as many beautiful women as they want, never once having to risk being rejected.

But Mitch's situation was extreme. Unlike most men who use pornography as an occasional reprieve from continually having to risk rejection, Mitch used it as a substitute for human contact. The only way he would ever be able to have sex with a woman (instead of a fantasy object) was to stop being paralyzed by his fear of rejection—of being kicked out and locked out from the source of love, comfort, and security.

Mitch and I talked about his need to face his fears. He no longer retreated to his fantasy that women would naturally come to him as they did in the movies. Even though Mitch now realized he would have to be a participant and not just an observer, his fear of rejection remained. He still felt paralyzed by this fear.

The best way to confront paralyzing fears is through a gradual, step-by-step process. So, I suggested as a first step placing a personal ad in a singles magazine. With this method, rejection remains somewhat removed from the person. Personal ads are appealing for just this reason. Mitch liked the idea of a personal ad but was very unsure of how it should be worded. He felt fairly certain that no woman would be interested in a thirty-six-year-old virgin but didn't want to meet a woman under false pretenses. Eventually, she would learn about his problem. Then not only would he be humiliated, but certainly she would leave. That wouldn't help him learn to face rejection, he argued.

I countered with the suggestion of an ad that admitted to his inexperience. At first he was very opposed, still believing that nobody would want a sexually inexperienced man. I threw out the idea that perhaps an inexperienced man might be appealing to an inexperienced woman.

"You mean neither one of us would know what to do? That doesn't sound so great to me," he responded.

"It happens all the time, Mitch. It's just that it usually happens at a much younger age. I really believe that there are many women out there who are just as frightened as you are—women who have avoided sexual experience for the same reasons as you. I'm betting they would welcome the opportunity to take it slowly, to work through the fears together. It would take a great deal of pressure off both of you to know ahead of time that you're both in the same boat."

"But what if she's ugly? Then what do I do?"

"Your fixation on having the perfect woman has been just another way for you to avoid rejection. By insisting on perfection you eliminate all real possibilities."

"But I'm not sure I'll get turned on if she doesn't look like the women in the movies."

"Think about it, Mitch. Getting turned on is really the least of your worries. First you have to learn to be comfortable just talking to a woman. Think about how afraid you were when you first met Angel. Eventually that fear went away. The more women you meet, even if sex is never a part of it, the more comfortable you'll become. Besides, you'll find that sexual desire is a natural outcome of feeling connected to another person."

"Being connected to another person—that's a feeling I've never had. At one time I thought I was connected to Angel, but now I realize it was really one-sided. She was never really interested in me, only in herself . . . . For a long time I guess I felt that way about you too—that you didn't really care about me."

"It's hard for you to believe that anyone could really care about you, Mitch. As a result of your feeling both kicked out and locked out, you unknowingly decided that no one could be trusted to care. It was much safer—less painful—for you not to let anybody in."

"But I can see now that nothing will change unless I begin to risk . . . you know, let someone in. Do you really think I'd get an answer to an ad that says 'Inexperienced male seeks inexperienced female to explore the possibilities of love'?"

Mitch did get some answers to his ad. He didn't immediately fall in love or lose his virginity. But he did take a woman to dinner, go to the theater with a woman, walk on the beach with a woman, and even make out on the couch with a woman. About a year or so after he left therapy, I received a note in the mail from him. All it said was *Bingo!*

JACQUELINE

THE BROKEN CONVENANT

This story begins with a gathering of people whose collective past paints a heartbreaking picture. I'm speaking of the world of the ex-drug addict. With drugs, as with a hurricane, there is always a quiet before the storm when life seems peaceful, even friendly. Inevitably, like a hurricane, drugs erupt, destroying everything and everyone in their path.

As a therapist I have known many ex-addicts. But it was a personal friendship, not a professional relationship, that led me to attend an Alcoholics Anonymous meeting. In support of my friend's courage, I attended her tenth-anniversary celebration of sobriety. It was not my first AA meeting, and yet, at this point in my life, it did turn into a first.

It's virtually impossible to be a therapist and not deal with some form of addiction in one's clients. So, early in my career I attended several AA meetings as a means of familiarizing myself with the program. I was a young, inexperienced therapist and did it more out of duty than for any personal commitment to my own growth. Consequently, I walked away from those few meetings with a detached, professional appreciation for the recovering alcoholic.

Now, years later, sitting in this particular meeting, I had a different feeling altogether. What made it different for me now was that, as a seasoned therapist, I had been privileged to know intimately the trials and victories of many people who had kicked the habit. And my personal friendship with one of these truly courageous people brought it even closer to home. So, as I looked around the room at the veteran faces of triumph over tragedy, this time I felt a deep-rooted, respectful appreciation toward the immense variety of people who were linked together by this common thread.

I was so engrossed in my periscopic behavior that I was momentarily startled when my eyes connected with the eyes of an attractive man sitting a few rows ahead of me. He had to turn his body to see me, so I felt certain he was intentionally trying to make eye contact. But as soon as we did connect, he immediately looked away. In that single moment of connection, I felt beseeched by those eyes, as if he was calling out a challenge to me to figure him out. I looked at him several times throughout the remaining meeting, but he didn't turn around again. As people were leaving, I pointed him out to my friend and asked her about him.

"Do you know that man over there?" I asked. The slim one with the Paul Newman eyes?"

"Yes," she said. "Isn't he cute? All the single women in this room would give their right arm to go out with him. A few have even tried to get him to ask them out, but he's aloof. Even though he comes to almost every meeting, he rarely talks to anyone, and he never attends anything social. We wonder if he isn't gay—probably because it makes us feel better to believe that than to believe he doesn't find us interesting.''

''There is something about him that's very compelling,'' I commented, ''but I don't know exactly what it is.''

''Unless you enjoy trying to melt an iceberg, I suggest you forget about *that* man,'' she warned.

And I did forget about him until about ten days later when a new patient showed up in my office. This new patient, a very tall, slender, somewhat overly made-up but sexy woman with a throaty voice, seemed vaguely familiar to me. When I mentioned this to her she said she had seen me at the AA meeting.

''I thought sure you wouldn't remember me,'' she said, ''since you seemed so preoccupied by the man a few rows ahead of you.''

I felt that very uncomfortable feeling one gets when caught with one's hand in the cookie jar, so to speak. She's got the goods on me, I thought, so there's no point in denying it. ''Yes, I guess I was staring at him. I thought him interesting,'' I confessed.

''Did you really?'' she asked emphatically.

''Yes, I did. Do you know him?''

She didn't answer me at first. Instead, she stared at me as if trying to make a decision. Finally, she said, ''Not really, I guess. He's difficult to know.''

''That seems to be the consensus of a number of women.''

''Yes, I know,'' she said flatly, signaling to an end to this line of discussion.

''So, tell me about yourself, Jacqueline.''

''What do you want to know?'' she asked.

My theory on getting to know patients has always been to let the patient set the direction. Where they start and what they choose to talk about is important because it tells me a lot about them. It is information I might not get if I guided the conversation with questions. So, I replied the way I always do when I get this question from a patient: ''I want to know whatever you feel like telling me.''

''Well, I'm not sure why I'm here. I mean I don't think anyone can really help me with my problem. I want to stop feeling like I don't belong, but I've been living with it for so long now it seems like an impossible goal. When I was a girl, I tried religion. At first it seemed like that was working, but in the end it seemed to make the problems worse. Then, as a teenager, I dealt with it by drinking. I can look back on it now and see I was an alcoholic by the time I was sixteen. I'm forty-three now and have been sober for four years. Being sober is often tougher than being a drunk, you know.'' She had been looking off into space but turned her eyes toward me when she spoke the last sentence.

''I'd probably still be a drunk if I hadn't botched my own suicide attempt. Five years ago I drove my car into a concrete wall. Funny part was I wasn't even drunk at the time. I ended up in the hospital for almost a year. Of course, I couldn't keep my alcohol habit going in the hospital, and toward the end of my stay I spent some time in an alcohol rehab program. I don't know why I stay sober. Every day of my life is pure hell.

''Before I got sober, I led a double life. By day, I was a successful businesswoman, by night a procurer of sex. Do you remember that movie, *Looking for Mr. Goodbar?* Well, that was me. At least when I was drunk, I felt like I was having some enjoyment in life. Most nights I'd sit at a bar and have a few drinks until some man would come over and offer to buy me some more drinks. It almost never failed that some man would try to pick me up. Anyway, by the time I was good and drunk, I was ready to hop in the sack with just about anyone, so it didn't matter much to me. Of course it wasn't all fun and games. There were several times I got beat up badly by the jerk-of-the-evening. You'd think that would teach me a lesson, but I'd be back at it as soon as the bruises could be covered by makeup.

143

"I've found that to stay sober, I have to stay out of the bars. Without the bars, there was no sex. It was only then that it became clear to me that I was addicted to both the alcohol and the sex. You know, it's okay in AA to talk about almost anything you've done—except sex, that is. Nobody talks about sex. I mean, in a group of recovered alcoholics, you'd be hard pressed to rate the humiliating things we've done, so no one bothers to make judgments. But talking about sex is different—it remains a taboo subject.

"Your ears must have been burning at that AA meeting because people were passing it around that you were a sex therapist. That's how I found out about you. I'd never seen a sex therapist, and I didn't realize it until I saw you, but I guess I thought sex therapists had two heads or something. When I saw you were okay . . . you know, normal, I thought it must be a sign of some sort. Actually, I've known all my adult life that I needed some help. Things have never been right with me sexually, but I've been too afraid to face it. Alcohol allowed me to run away from my fear. Of course, it created an entirely new set of problems. It always does. Anyway, if you hadn't been at that meeting, I'd still be running away."

I was furiously taking notes as Jacqueline talked. In an emotionally flat tone of voice she was casually and rapidly firing crisis after crisis at me: alcoholism, a suicide attempt, sexual addiction, self-destructive behavior. And we were only halfway through the session. I didn't know exactly what I had on my hands with this woman, but I knew her case would be complex. It would take months just to put all the pieces of the puzzle on the table. I hadn't spoken in quite a while, but she didn't seem to notice. Instead, she went on as if she had pretaped what she wanted to say and had simply pushed the button and was sitting back listening to the sound of her own voice.

"Ever since I can remember," she continued, "the first thought I had each morning when I awoke was that I didn't belong in the world. That somehow I'd been a mistake. It was a very scary feeling."

For the first time since she started talking, I felt a need to clarify something she said. "You said as early as you can remember you felt that way. Would you say that was before you started school?" I asked.

"It's always been such a part of my life that it feels like I was *born* thinking that."

I took particular note of this last remark. It's not unusual for unwanted children to feel the way Jacqueline just described. So I asked her if she knew whether her parents planned to have her.

"Yes and no," she answered. "You see, I have five brothers. My mother really wanted a girl so I guess she got pregnant again without talking about it with my dad. I remember lots of fights about it. I don't think my dad really wanted any children, and he ended up with six. But my mother was so thrilled to have a girl, she favored me over my brothers. This caused lots of fights.

"Somewhere between child number four and number six my dad started drinking. I mean there was a lot of commotion in our home, and Dad couldn't take it so he'd start drinking as soon as he walked into the house. Of course, that only added to the commotion because then Mom and Dad would start fighting."

Jacqueline went on like this for the rest of the session and many after as well. The more I listened to her story, the more I knew I had been right in my first impression: Her life history was complex—and extremely chaotic. In summary, here's what I learned.

The chaos of Jacqueline's life actually had two recurrent themes: loud, angry fighting and her feeling of not belonging. There were fights between her mom and dad, fights between her brothers, and fights between her dad and her brothers. Jacqueline, frightened by all the fighting, would hide under the bed and cover her ears during the shouting matches.

Jacqueline was raised on a farm in the South. And while her family didn't have much money, they weren't as poor as many of the other children who lived on surrounding farms. The Baptist church was predominant in her community, and Jacqueline's mother was a devout member of the local church. Her father shunned religion, presenting one more battleground for the two of them.

Being her mother's favorite, Jacqueline would proudly accompany her mother to Sunday worship services. Later, when she was older, she attended Bible classes, and her Bible became her constant companion. She prided herself on the fact that she had many parts of it memorized. It was her Bible she turned to for comfort when things would get chaotic in the house, especially when her parents would fight. Now too old to hide under the bed, she would take her Bible with her to the barn and wait out the storm.

Hiding was something Jacqueline became accustomed to, not only because of the fighting between her parents but because her brothers took great joy in teasing her unmercifully. They resented the special attention lavished on her by their mother, and they were always calling her "mamma's baby." Jacqueline's defense was to find ways to avoid them as much as possible. She was good at becoming invisible, but with five brothers around, it seemed like she was always running into one or another of them when she least expected it. She hated it when she'd open a door or turn a corner to find one or more of them lurking around. She knew she was in for it, and likely as not, she'd end up in tears. It never occurred to Jacqueline to fight back—she hated fighting too much. And she didn't dare tell her mother because she knew that would mean retribution at a later time. Anyway, her mother never really had any control over the boys. And no matter how much yelling her father did, it didn't seem like he could handle them either. To Jacqueline, her brothers seemed wild and totally out of control.

As an adult Jacqueline rarely had contact with any of her brothers. One of them—the meanest in her mind—continued to be a mean "son-of-a-bitch" as an adult. He currently was in jail on a robbery charge and had served previous sentences as well for petty theft. Jacqueline hadn't seen him in fifteen years. Two others grew up to be addicted to alcohol; both were divorced and still drinking, as far as she knew. The other two seemed more "normal" to Jacqueline. Both were married and had families, but both were still prone to violent tempers, and Jacqueline felt sorry for their families.

We spent many weeks talking about her unhappy youth and her retreat from the ugly world she lived in. When she was a little girl, her mother would read to her at bedtime from the Bible. Jacqueline would fall asleep feeling the peacefulness of her mother's voice and the reassurance that the Lord would watch over her. But her dreams were anything but peaceful. During the dark of the night, she felt God slip away, and by morning she awoke with the same feelings of dread, fear, and not belonging. Nonetheless, she always slept with her Bible under her pillow, hoping that somehow it would keep God with her during the night.

When she was still a little girl, she tried to talk to her mother about her fears, but her mother told her to put her faith in the Lord and he would comfort her. He truly cared about and watched over all good people, her mother said. This only made Jacqueline wonder even more why he wasn't watching over her. She concluded it must be because she wasn't a good person. So she tried even harder to be a good girl and to do all the things the Bible commanded her to do.

If it wasn't for her brothers, she felt things might have changed and she could have become a good person. But her brothers were always getting in the way of her attempts to do good. They mocked her all the time and called her names. She didn't understand these names, but they didn't sound like ones that belonged to a good person. She knew from her Bible lessons that good people didn't hate others. But she hated her brothers. Each morning before she got out of bed she would wonder how to solve her dilemma: How was it possible to follow the Lord's commandments with hate in her heart?

When she entered school, she found that the other children treated her very much like her brothers did. They shunned her and the older ones called her the same names that her brothers called her. Jacqueline's response was to retreat further and further into herself and into her Bible. She believed that somewhere in her treasured book was the answer to the question of how she could change and become a good person.

But she never found the answer in her Bible. What did change things for Jacqueline had nothing to do with words and had everything to do with her body. It seemed sudden to Jacqueline, but as she entered the seventh grade, her body started acting very strangely. Of most importance was that she started to get tall, taller than most of the other kids in her class. This caused a sudden change in the response of a few of her classmates. She vividly remembered how one of them approached her and asked her if she had ever considered playing basketball. Jacqueline had never thought about sports, and she didn't have the slightest idea if she would be any good, but it felt so great to be asked that she said she would think it over.

Her mother was emphatically opposed to Jacqueline's playing basketball, but her father encouraged her. It was the first time Jacqueline could remember her father encouraging her about anything. She only wondered mildly why he even bothered to care. (She had given up on him years before.) Her goal had always been to stay out of his way. However, she remembered well the fight that ensued between her parents when he insisted that she play ball. Jacqueline worried for days about defying her mother. She had never opposed her mother's wishes before, but she so desperately wanted to belong to a group—any group—that she disobeyed her mother for the first time in her life. This decision was a turning point in her life.

She surprised herself by being a well-coordinated and agile ball player. But the most important part of it was that for the first time in her life she had friends. These friends, however, were not at all interested in religion or the Bible. They were more interested in having a good time, and drinking was always a part of having a good time. Jacqueline claimed to remember little about her period of trans-formation except to say that with her friends and with alcohol she found peace of mind. The fears that had felt like a ball and chain were finally gone, releasing her to a world that seemed accepting instead of rejecting. She was willing to pay whatever price was necessary to be free from those fears.

By the time she reached high school, her height was no longer that unusual. And at this level of play, her coordi-nation couldn't overcome her biggest drawback: lack of ag-gression. She made the team but ended up warming the bench most of the year. She didn't even bother trying out the following year.

By then she had already established her "crowd," fur-ther deteriorating the once-tranquil relationship with her mother. All her brothers except one had left home as quickly as possible. For years Jacqueline had looked forward to her brothers' leaving, believing there would be less fighting in the house. But now the fights were between Jacqueline and her mother. The peacefulness that Jacqueline had dreamed about never materialized, and she bitterly recalled her mother's loud voice lamenting, "What's become of my sweet little princess?"

But Jacqueline found the feelings of belonging to a group more compelling than bending to her mother's will. She had always been a compliant child, trying to please her mother in order to feel loved. Her mother had promised her that the Lord would give her peace. She remembered her mother's frequent quoting of Leviticus 26:3 & 6: "If ye walk in my statutes, and keep my commandments, and do them, And I will give you peace in the land, and ye shall lie down, and none shall make you afraid; and I will rid evil beasts out of the land. . . ." Even though she had tried to follow his commandments, she had never been protected from her evil brothers. It wasn't the Lord who took away her fears, it was belonging . . . and it was alcohol.

So when Jacqueline graduated from high school, she left home just like all her brothers before her. Unlike her brothers, however, she went on to a junior college and studied business. While in school she got a part-time job with an insurance company and learned claims adjusting. After several years with the company she started selling insurance and eventually went on to be one of their top performers. It was during these years she led what she called her "double life."

I had known Jacqueline several months now, and I still didn't know much about her sexual development. Other than what she read in the Bible, she claimed there was no discussion about sex either at home or in school. As a teenager she never really dated, preferring instead to hang out with her select group of friends. Her first sexual experience came after she left home. While in college she met a boy in one of her classes. According to Jacqueline they dated only briefly. "He was really pushy about sex," she said. "I wasn't that interested in him, but I wanted to get the first time over with, so I went to bed with him. I don't remember much about it so I guess it wasn't anything special."

In some ways, Jacqueline's lack of recall around her sexual development was typical. Few of us can remember where we learned about sexuality because so much of it is indirectly acquired. Unless we've had some extremely traumatic experiences that we can remember, most of us learn about sex through a silent process of cultural osmosis and, later, through simple trial and error. Most religions, however, are not at all silent about the sanctioned boundaries of sex.

So, I was surprised by the way Jacqueline downplayed any religious influence on her developing sexuality. And I was surprised by her denial that any sexual activity occurred during her teenage drinking years. Teenage drinking and early sexual activity usually go hand in hand. Given the self-destructive way Jacqueline used sex, it was likely that something powerfully negative had influenced her early sexual development and that she was blocking the memory of what it was.

Although Jacqueline believed it was true, her unhealthy use of sex as an adult didn't *suddenly* emerge out of the blue. Something deep inside her was driving her to act in compulsive ways. Risking her health and life, for no profit, by picking up strange men on a regular basis is not behavior that is motivated by an intact, sound ego. Nor is suicidal behavior.

In fact, my impression over the months that I had known Jacqueline was that she was operating with an extremely fragile ego. There was a dark, secretive side of her that was hidden even from herself. I felt this way because she continued to present her history in a rather matter-of-fact way. And yet, the problem was she was describing was anything but matter-of-fact.

Not only did I feel her ego was fragile, but also I felt our relationship was equally vulnerable. I didn't feel Jacqueline was letting me make a connection with her. Each week she would remind me that she didn't think therapy would really help and that she didn't know why she was even bothering. Every once in a while she would cancel an appointment, and even though she rescheduled, I was never sure she would show up. She reminded me of an orphaned cub left to deal with the vicissitudes of the jungle, poised to bolt at the slightest indication of danger.

Yet, I was sure there was much more to this woman than what I could see on the surface. Her outside appearance was deceptive. Each time I saw her she was dressed immaculately. Her makeup—which I thought excessive—was perfectly done, as was her hair. Her clothing was always feminine, never tailored, and she always presented herself as the perfect lady. Her emotions were understated and controlled. Even when she talked about the brothers she despised, she did so with flat affect.

Although I felt there were many aspects of Jacqueline's history that were still undiscovered, I sensed that both her fragile ego and our weak relationship would not take pushing. So I stopped asking questions about her history and waited to see what Jacqueline would do. Before I could find out, there was an unexpected turn of events.

It started with a telephone call from a stranger who claimed to be a "friend" of Jacqueline's. Before she would say anything, however, she wanted to know that, if she came in for an appointment, our conversation would be confidential. She didn't want Jacqueline to know she had been to see me.

Jacqueline hadn't mentioned any particular friends, but then Jacqueline hadn't spoken much about her current personal life at all, except to say she continued to feel she didn't belong. Her one social venture was to attend AA meetings, and even there she isolated herself.

"I don't think it would be a good idea because as Jacqueline's therapist, I shouldn't have any secrets from her. Secrets jeopardize trust," I told her, "and therapy is built around trust."

The unidentified stranger then said, "There's something you need to know about Jacqueline if you're going to help."

"It's up to Jacqueline to tell me what I need to know," I responded quickly. I was afraid this woman was going to tell me her secret anyway.

"Well, Jacqueline won't tell you," she said sharply. "Jacqueline won't tell anybody."

"Can I tell Jacqueline you called?"

"No, that would ruin things between us. But you need to know this about her."

I could tell that if I didn't quickly end this conversation, I would find myself exactly where I didn't want to be. "I'm sorry, but I'm going to have to end this conversation. I appreciate your concern for Jacqueline, but it's really best if you tell your concerns to Jacqueline, not me. I just can't help Jacqueline if I have to keep secrets from her." I hung up the phone, hoping the woman wouldn't call me back. I didn't want to be in the middle of whatever it was that was going on between the two of them.

Of course, ignoring a phone call is like asking a jury to disregard testimony: Once you've heard it, it's difficult to forget you know it. Consequently, the next time I saw Jacqueline, I wondered how this person fit into her life. She had never mentioned having any special friend. In fact, Jacqueline's theme had always been her feeling of not belonging, of never being really close to anybody.

Just at the moment I was entertaining these thoughts, Jacqueline said, "My friend told me she called you."

It's at times like this that I not only believe in the possibility of ESP but can see the potential benefits. I breathed a sigh of relief because it was now out in the open and no longer a threat to the trust between us.

"What exactly did she tell you about the call?" I asked.

"She told me you wouldn't talk to her."

"Did she tell you why?"

"She said you told her it was up to me to tell you about me."

"Yes, that's what I said."

"I was really angry at her for calling. Although she doesn't agree, I think my therapy is my business, not hers."

"Do you know why she doesn't agree?"

"Yes." Then silence.

I was hoping to get more and I knew that Jacqueline knew I wanted more. But she was quiet, so I remained quiet.

Jacqueline stared off into space, lost in her private thoughts. Finally, she turned her eyes toward mine and spoke. "We're lovers. She thinks you ought to know."

There were tears in Jacqueline's eyes, indicating that this admission was in some way painful to her. Since she had hidden this information from me until this point, I sensed a strong component of shame in her admission.

"This is painful for you, isn't it?"

"Yes. It feels like a confession. You know, like I've been living in sin."

"Perhaps that's what your self-destructive behavior has been all about. A way to punish yourself for what you perceive to be sinful behavior."

"I wish I wasn't gay, but I can't seem to control it. I mean, I would go for months without a lover and instead would spend time in the bars. Eventually, however, I would take another female lover and try to make the relationship work, only to sabotage the relationship within a few months. The relationship I'm in now has lasted the longest of any. It's lasted almost three years, but it hasn't been easy. Every day I feel the need to run away from it. I thought therapy might help me keep from ruining this one as well. But when I got in here, I couldn't bring myself to tell you I was in a homosexual relationship. If she hadn't called, I'd probably never have told you."

"How do you feel now that you have?"

"Better. It's like a weight lifted off my shoulders."

This disclosure explained many things to me about Jacqueline. Now I knew why I had sensed a dark, secretive side of her. The shame and guilt she felt drove her to act compulsively to counteract her homosexual urges, thus the repetitive picking up of men in the bars. However, her compulsive attempts to drive away her homosexual impulses failed. With enough failures under her belt, suicide seemed to her an easier solution than facing the feelings of failure.

And I now understood why she kept our relationship so at bay. She feared rejection from me should I discover her secret. Yet she asked herself how therapy could help if she didn't tell me the truth. So therapy had added conflict, not subtracted it from Jacqueline's life. And more conflict certainly wasn't what Jacqueline needed. Obviously, she had been living all her adult life with conflict over her sexual preferences. This could easily explain why she had a strong feeling of not belonging.

I was still puzzled, however, as to why she described this feeling of not belonging as *always* being there. That part of it still didn't make sense to me. Most likely there were still pieces of her history missing that would shed some light on her feelings of not belonging.

The cause of homosexual behavior remains unknown. We do know that hormones during pregnancy influence sex differences in behavior and language. But hormones alone do not explain sexual preferences. Cultural traditions play an extremely important role in determining how these hormonal differences will be manifested.

In our culture, homosexual feelings are often accompanied by feelings of not being accepted. This would make sense because of the majority belief that heterosexual behavior is normal and that any deviation from the norm constitutes abnormal behavior. It's interesting to note, however, that this isn't true in all cultures. What is normal may be defined differently according to the traditions of different societies.

Anthropological studies have shown that certain cultures in western Sumatra, southern New Guinea, and eastern Melanesian Pacific Islands actually prescribe homosexuality for males in the period between puberty and parenthood and forbid heterosexual relationships apart from marriage and parenthood as a way for young males to release sexual tension prior to marriage. Heterosexual relationships are allowed only after marriage. The purpose of this cultural mandate is to ensure that young women will be virgins until married, while at the same time recognizing the emerging sexual needs of the males. (The emerging sexual needs of the females are apparently not considered.) Marriage is the first and only heterosexual partnership, and once the men are married, homosexual behavior is simply discontinued in favor of heterosexual sex.

If biology alone explained homosexuality, it would be impossible for human beings to adhere to it then abandon it, all according to tradition. So, after learning this new information about Jacqueline, I was more convinced than ever that I didn't have a complete picture of all that had happened to her as a child. There was, indeed, much more to learn, and I was feeling optimistic that she would be more open with me now that she had revealed her previously guarded secret and discovered she would not be abandoned.

It took several more sessions for Jacqueline to begin to trust that I would not reject her because of her recent disclosure. Eventually she began to talk about her earliest homosexual feelings. She remembered having strange sexual feelings during the times she hid in the barn to escape the fighting. She couldn't remember any of the details, only that something unusual happened during those times and that it was somehow related to her current feelings. While the specifics were unavailable to her, she definitely could recall the feeling that "things weren't right." There was, however, a particular part of those many episodes of hiding in the barn she could remember. It had to do with her Bible.

She always took the Bible with her when she went to hide. She couldn't recall actually reading it while hiding, but she did remember several incidents of leaving the barn with her Bible in hand. It felt hot, like it had been in a fire, and her eyes burned, as if by reading it she had singed her eyes. After each of these experiences she could recall feeling like she was in a daze, and it would take an hour or more for her eyes to stop burning.

It was when she started playing basketball that she could first clearly remember having homosexual desires. To Jacqueline it all seem to start innocently when two girls on the team invited her to attend a party. At first she just thought they were being friendly, and after years of being without friends, their invitation felt good. There was alcohol at their "party," which ended up consisting of just the three girls. They acted silly and laughed a lot. Eventually, however, their get-togethers involved physical touching. It was very scary at first, but Jacqueline was too inhibited to refuse, too afraid she might lose her friends if she did. She went along with their suggestions, followed their directions, and soon discovered a pleasure she had never dreamed of. The "parties" became a regular occurrence.

After each interlude, the guilt she felt was overwhelming. She promised herself she wouldn't get involved in any more of their parties but couldn't seem to keep her promise. She knew she was breaking all the rules outlined in her beloved Bible and that she must quit before she was damned to hell forever. Still, she couldn't stay away. With the girls she felt like she belonged, and the pleasure from their sexual encounters was so enormous that she questioned how it was possible for it to be wrong. Instead of staying away from her new friends, she stayed away from religion. It was then that the fights with her mother began.

The threesome remained together through their first year in high school. But then one of the girls started dating a boy. This was total betrayal in Jacqueline's mind, and the hurt she felt was unlike anything she'd ever experienced. The girls started fighting among themselves, and eventually the friendship fell apart completely. Without her two friends, Jacqueline felt lost. The feelings of not belonging returned and Jacqueline turned to alcohol for consolation—it deadened the pain she felt. Making new friends seemed out of the question because Jacqueline now knew she was different from the others and wouldn't be accepted. She had no interest at all in boys, nor did they seem to have any interest in her.

After high school she had one date with a boy but it felt creepy, especially when he got a little too friendly. Then, about two years after she graduated, she met her first real lover. Her name was Micky. With Micky the sex felt right. They made joyous, passionate love that lasted for hours. It was during these times Jacqueline felt like she belonged. So she was puzzled by the fact that within several months she started feeling restless about the relationship. She didn't know why, but it stopped feeling right. Even alcohol couldn't make it feel right. She felt terribly confused. How could something that felt so right also feel so wrong?

It was then that she ended up cruising the bars. She found that if she drank enough, she could enjoy taking a man to bed. She had no idea why she did this; she only knew she felt compelled to do it. When Micky eventually found out what Jacqueline was doing when she stayed out all night, she broke off the relationship. Jacqueline felt a pain similar to the one she had experienced in high school when her friend "betrayed" her. But she experienced something else that confused her even more. She also felt relieved when Micky walked out. If she didn't want Micky, why did it hurt so much when she left? She didn't know the answer to this question.

She never did find the answer. Instead, she repeated this pattern over and over again. Sometimes she would go for years and never have a relationship. During these times she would remain celibate. Then, she would start a new relationship with a woman, only to feel a restlessness start to grow inside her just when things were going well. The restlessness drove her to the bars. Her lovers would always find out what she was doing. Some of them would stay for a while, choosing to believe she would stop tormenting them with her promiscuous behavior. In spite of their pleas, she never stopped picking up men. If they elected to stay, Jacqueline would find ways to pick fights with them so that she could avoid any sexual contact. Eventually, she would make life so miserable for them that out of desperation they would leave.

After they were gone, Jacqueline would experience the same terrible feelings of loneliness she felt after Micky left, but she would always experience the same feelings of relief as well. During the times when Jacqueline was without a lover, she would concentrate all her energy on her work. She was making excellent money selling commercial insurance and worked mostly on her own schedule. She could easily complete her work within half a day. Unfortunately, this gave her time to drink during the day, and in her late thirties, she was drinking heavily by the time the sun was setting.

Then it all started to catch up with her. She began missing appointments with clients, or drinking too much when she took them to lunch, or she was never available to service the accounts she had. Slowly, she began losing accounts. Her personal life had always been a mass of confusion, pain, and failure, but her work had brought her success. Now it, too, was crumbling down around her.

With perfect clarity of mind, she remembered her decision to end it all. She was driving back from a morning appointment, thinking about what a mess she had made of her life. Most of her life she had felt she didn't belong. It now seemed really very simple. She would just take herself out of this life where she never belonged in the first place. With these thoughts in her head, she drove her car straight into a freeway overpass.

At the moment of impact, she felt something she realized she had been searching for all her life: freedom. After that she remembered nothing until she awoke in the emergency room of a hospital, surrounded by doctors and nurses. Then she immediately lost consciousness again. The next thing she remembered was waking up in the intensive care unit.

She had multiple fractures and some internal injuries that had needed surgery, but, remarkably, there was little serious damage. The doctors said she was lucky, but to Jacqueline living meant feeling trapped in an alien soul; life was not a blessing.

Because of her multiple fractures, she had casts on almost every part of her body. It was ironic, she thought, how much this symbolized her feeling of being trapped. Although the casts would eventually disappear, Jacqueline knew her feeling of being trapped would not. She lay there day after day, wondering how it was that she could be such a misfit and a failure. To make matters worse, she was forced to dry out. The alcohol had at least provided momentary peace in the battle going on inside her. Without it there was full-scale war.

Jacqueline was visited regularly by an alcohol-dependency counselor, but she resisted his attempts to reach her. It was easy to admit she had an alcohol problem, but she could never tell this man about her double life. She didn't feel she could tell anyone; increasing her feelings of being an aberration.

She was in the hospital for almost a year and then was transferred to the alcoholic rehabilitation unit for six weeks. She attended all the group meetings and listened to what the counselors and other patients had to say, but she never once felt like she belonged to the group. She was forced to admit to herself, however, that if she wanted her career back, she'd have to stay sober. After her discharge, she joined AA and began to build her business again. It was slow going, and she had to live very differently without the financial cushion she had built before. Every single day she wondered why she even bothered. She went through life feeling mechanical, as if some greater power wound her up each morning, operating automatically and without thought. She was faithful about attending AA, only because she knew that if she didn't, she'd be committing *slow* suicide. She thought often about suicide but knew that if she was going to do it, she would do it quickly and *right* this time.

The only human contact Jacqueline had, other than her clients, was with her physical therapist. Because of all the fractures, she had to have frequent therapy sessions. There was a lot of physical contact in these sessions. There had been a lot of physical contact in the hospital as well. Jacqueline had hated this requirement. Virtually helpless with all her casts, she had to be fed, turned, lifted onto a bedpan—it was degrading and invasive. But physical therapy was different. Her therapist, a woman, was good-natured and always joking with Jacqueline. In contrast to her, Jacqueline felt like a bitch, grouchy and irritable. The woman seemed undaunted by her bad moods and continued to joke with Jacqueline, teasing her about being a grouch.

Jacqueline began looking forward to her sessions. It was a new and strange feeling. An excited anticipation started to grow inside Jacqueline before each meeting with Samantha. She knew from the past that this was a dangerous feeling. It was dangerous from all angles. If the woman didn't have the same sexual inclinations as Jacqueline, she would be insulted and probably refuse to see Jacqueline again. Even though Jacqueline was very coy about her "invitations" to women, she had made mistakes in the past, misreading certain behaviors and ending up with hurtful rejections. It would also be dangerous if the woman was interested in a sexual relationship. Jacqueline felt sure she would simply repeat her pattern, ultimately finding a way to ruin the relationship. But without alcohol, sex with men seemed an impossibility to Jacqueline. She no longer had an escape route if she needed it. In some ways this frightened her, but in another way she thought it might be good— maybe she would be forced once and for all to face her fears about relationships.

Although all of these thoughts caused Jacqueline great anxiety, she found her irritability disappearing when she was around Samantha. Instead, she turned on the charm.

For reasons Jacqueline never understood, turning on the charm always worked. Flirting with women had always been easy for her. She just had to be sure she read the cues right. It was difficult to read Samantha, however, because she had this extroverted quality about her. She always seemed friendly and genuinely interested in Jacqueline. But as the months passed, Jacqueline began to feel more and more certain that she could extend a social invitation to Samantha and it would be accepted.

It took her weeks to get up the courage, but she had been unable to think about anything else, and she knew she had to do something about it to keep from going crazy. Her fears, as usual, were for naught. Samantha, like most of the women before her, responded with delight. Also, as before, the relationship started out well, but, inevitably, Jacqueline started to feel the restlessness; only now, as feared, she didn't have the alcohol and the bars as an escape route. And Samantha was different from the women before her. Unlike the others, she responded to Jacqueline's restlessness with support and caring instead of insecurity and possessiveness, and the relationship had lasted long past any of the others. Still, Jacqueline continued to feel a strong need to escape. Consequently, she would get moody and pick fights with Samantha, hoping to get her angry enough to leave.

Originally, it had been Samantha's idea for Jacqueline to go into therapy. Many of the other women had said the same thing, but it wasn't until Samantha that Jacqueline even entertained the idea. Then there had been the AA meeting that I attended, and that solidified the idea in Jacqueline's mind.

I now had a much clearer picture of Jacqueline. Yet there were still many unanswered questions, not the least of which was why Jacqueline felt so early in life that she didn't belong. And there was the issue of her repeated pattern of restlessness with her lovers. What was driving her to pull back? I wondered. What was it she feared?

Being comfortable with long-term intimacy in adulthood is often linked to effective bonding in the early mother-child relationship. Lack of effective bonding sentences a child to a lifetime of fear—a fear that love won't be returned. As a protection against the realization of this fear, the person never allows a real connection to continue. But Jacqueline described her mother as adoring of her, treating her as the special child because she was the desperately wanted girl. She should have felt secure and very wanted. Could her father (and her malevolent brothers) have counteracted the positive feelings coming from her mother? It might be possible, but for some reason I couldn't yet explain, I didn't think Jacqueline was telling me the entire truth about her relationship with her mother.

There was also something puzzling about her homosexual preference. The lack of bonding with her father and the overidentification with her mother could easily have made her vulnerable to homosexual feelings. To Jacqueline, men (as represented by her father and brothers) were abusive, mean, and not to be trusted. Women, on the other hand, were accepting, warm, and loving. But why then would she need to pull away when the relationship was at its peak? And why choose sexual promiscuity as a way to do it? Obviously there were still parts of Jacqueline's life she either wasn't telling me or had blocked from her memory. I suspected that the undisclosed parts were sexual in nature, since she acted these out by being sexually promiscuous.

Additionally, it seemed strange to me that she claimed she had escaped any sex play with her siblings. An only girl growing up around five brothers was likely to have experienced *some* memorable sexual incidents. Yet Jacqueline couldn't remember anything at all. Her total loss of recall around this particular issue bothered me, acting as a warning flag to pay closer attention.

And then there was her early exposure to biblical instruction. The Bible is a complicated, discursive text that allows for variable interpretations. In an authoritarian voice, it commands its readers to comply, or else suffer damnation. As a therapist, I have often seen how the unsophisticated mind of a child misinterprets its dictates and how fear is instilled in the child at the thought of noncompliance. Being human, a child will eventually fail to follow its commandments perfectly. When this happens, the child experiences feelings of inadequacy and guilt that often stay with him or her for a lifetime.

All of these areas needed further exploration. Since Jacqueline's recall around these issues was skimpy, I had to try something to jar her memory. Jacqueline's only specific memories had to do with her Bible. She remembered hiding in the barn and afterward feeling as if her eyes were burning from reading it. And she remembered certain parts her mother used to quote. Since her only two specific memories had to do with the Bible, I thought this might be a way to trigger some lost memories. I asked her if she still owned the Bible she carried as a child. She was surprised by my question but said yes, she did. When I asked her if she would be willing to bring it in, she hesitated.

"I haven't looked at it in more than twenty-five years. It would feel strange to do it now."

"I think it could help us solve many of your unanswered questions."

"How is that?" she asked.

"It might trigger some memories for you."

"I'm not sure I want any more memories triggered. Just the idea of looking at it and touching it makes me feel weird."

"But that ought to tell you something, Jacqueline."

"Tell me what?"

"If you're feeling weird about it, that means there's something significant you're blocking that has to do with it."

"Well, I'll look for it," she said, but I detected little conviction in her voice and assumed she was just putting me off.

The next week when Jacqueline came in, she was slightly disheveled. It was noticeable on her only because she had always been immaculately put together on every other visit. I asked her if she had had a bad day, but she ignored my question. Instead, she said she had looked for her Bible but couldn't find it after all. There was something about the way she said it that made me question whether she was telling me the truth. I couldn't put my finger on what it was that made me feel that way, so I didn't say anything to her. She didn't say much to me either that day, and it was clear that she was distracted and unable to concentrate. When I pointed out that I thought she seemed distracted and asked again if there was something wrong, she replied negatively but didn't offer any explanation for her behavior. She watched the clock a lot that day and seemed relieved when the time was up.

As she was leaving, I said my usual "I'll see you next week." She turned toward me, looking at me as if she didn't know who I was or why I was making such a ridiculous remark. She didn't respond and just turned and walked out of my office in zombielike fashion.

Now I felt more convinced than ever that the Bible would provide us with some clues to Jacqueline's behavior. She had been resistant when I brought it up, and even though she had said she couldn't find it, her behavior indicated otherwise. I thought about bringing a Bible to our next session, but given her behavior in our last session, it seemed a risky thing to do. The whole idea had made her anxious, somehow interrupting her usual composure. Yet something was needed if we were to break through her defenses. The question in my mind was whether she was ready to be pushed to face something she feared greatly. If I was going to push, it would have to be done slowly because I just wasn't sure what ugliness we might find under the rock if we turned it over. And I certainly wasn't sure how Jacqueline might respond to its discovery.

A few days later I received an envelope in the mail. It contained a brief note along with a page torn out of the Bible. The note read, *Jacqueline still hasn't told you everything.* The page was from Leviticus 26. It wasn't signed, but I guessed it must have been from Samantha.

I studied the page I had received in the mail, carefully handling the yellowed, fragile paper. Could this be a page from Jacqueline's Bible, I wondered? And how much was Jacqueline sharing with Samantha? If Jacqueline hadn't told her about it, how could Samantha know that Jacqueline and I had been talking about the influence her early religious teachings had on her current life? Samantha's intent certainly must have been for me to pick up something that related to Jacqueline's life in what she sent. Perhaps Samantha was playing a game with me by providing me with clues. After all, I had told her not to give me direct information. It was obvious Samantha wanted to help and must have felt trapped between Jacqueline and me, since we were both telling her that Jacqueline's therapy was Jacqueline's business, not hers. Jacqueline had been adamant about not having Samantha join her in therapy or even see me separately. She didn't want Samantha to be a part of her therapy in any way.

Again, it occurred to me that there must be a clue, in the page I was holding, to an important missing piece of information. As I scanned the page, I immediately found the passage that Jacqueline had quoted to me earlier—the one she remembered her mother repeating about God providing peace in the land and ridding the land of evil, provided one kept his commandments. But I didn't think this was what I was supposed to discover because we had already talked about this part. I felt certain the intent was for me to discover something new—something Jacqueline had *not* told me.

The page was divided into sections. The part Jacqueline

remembered her mother quoting came from a section called "Conditions of blessing." The next section was titled "Warning of chastisement." This section told of the punishment for not following the Lord's commandments. I felt sure the answer to some of the missing pieces was contained in this section because there were several phrases that I easily connected to her hiding in the barn and afterward experiencing the burning pain. The passage read:

14 But if ye will not hearken unto me, and will not do all these commandments;

15 And if ye shall despise my statutes, or if your soul abhor mine ordinances, so that ye will not do all my commandments, but that ye break my convenant;

16 I also will do this unto you; I will even appoint over you terror, consumption, *and the burning fever, that shall consume the eyes, and cause sorrow of heart;* and ye shall sow your seed in vain, for your enemies shall eat it.

Instinctively, I knew there was a connection between the part about the burning fever and the burning sensation Jacqueline had described to me. Something terrible had happened in the barn—so terrible that she felt she had broken the Lord's commandments and was deserving of the punishment described. What painful experience was eluding her memory? I wondered. The answer must be contained in these passages. I read on:

17 And I will set my face against you, and ye shall be slain before your enemies; they that hate you shall reign over you, and ye shall *flee when none pursueth you.*

As I studied this passage, I began to see another connection—one between this passage and the relationship Jacqueline had with her brothers. Jacqueline had repeatedly described her brothers as her enemies, feeling that they hated her and were forever imposing a reign of terror over her life. She must have felt she had done something bad enough to *cause* her brothers to become her enemies. Whatever it was, she had blocked it out of her memory.

The very last part of Leviticus 17 shed light on the question both Jacqueline and I had been pondering. It explained to me why Jacqueline felt compelled to flee from her lovers—*ye shall flee when none pursueth you*, it said. Now it seemed evident to me that she felt undeserving of any happiness because God had commanded that she was unworthy and would feel fear where none existed.

Then, in proverbial light-bulb fashion, Jacqueline's life became clear to me: She had unknowingly been taking direction all these years from her Bible. She was literally acting out God's chastisement by punishing herself for breaking his commandments. It made more sense to me now why she would risk physical beating with unknown men; it was a form of self-flagellation. The fact that she had chosen sexual promiscuity as a way to find punishment convinced me more than ever that something sexual must have happened during those times when she was in the barn. And, no doubt, it had something to do with one or more of her brothers.

Had I not suspected that something sexual had happened between Jacqueline and one or more of her brothers, I probably wouldn't have found the clue I was searching for. But then I reread the last part of passage 16: . . . *and ye shall sow your seed in vain, for your enemies shall eat it*. In Biblical terms, *seed* is a euphemism for semen. Had her brother or brothers forced Jacqueline to perform oral sex on them? Was I leaping to conclusions? In the unquestioning mind of a child, could transgression have caused her brother or brothers to become her enemies?

If this was the psychological framework of her dilemma, in order to be free of her self-punishment, she would have to forgive herself for what she thought was her transgression against God. That meant that at some point, she would have to recall what it was she did that she thought so terrible. Yet our last session, even more than others, told me

Jacqueline was becoming less stable. Facing a painful memory might be too much for her. My pushing her toward the memory could easily boomerang and halt her progress. It would be better if she set the pace.

With the clues I had been given in the mail, I found myself in a very strange position vis-à-vis my patient: I knew something about her she didn't know. Usually it's the other way around; she is the only one who has access to the true story, even if it's buried so deep she doesn't have recall of it. I still wasn't exactly sure what I was going to do with this information. All I knew was that I must wait and see where Jacqueline took me next. It wasn't where I expected.

In our next session, Jacqueline acted very strangely. Her language was coarse, her manner sarcastic, even hostile at times. Gone was the perfect ladylike behavior I had become accustomed to, and in its place was the prototypical Amazon lady. I tried to find out what might have happened during the week to account for this change, but she kept denying that anything unusual had taken place.

I was uncertain as to how to proceed. I knew Jacqueline was under great stress. It seemed she had begun a slow transformation ever since I had brought up the idea of the Bible. In fact, her behavioral change was now so dramatic I entertained the idea that I just might be dealing with a multiple personality. It's true that genuine multiple personality is quite rare, but it's also true that it may go undiscovered and therefore undiagnosed. Most multiples have a history of severe childhood trauma so painful that they escape from the pain by becoming a new "person." If Jacqueline did have more than one personality inside of her, there was much more to learn about what exactly happened to her as a child.

Since I wasn't pushing Jacqueline at all, it must be something outside of our therapy sessions that was stressing her. I hadn't believed her when she first said she couldn't find her Bible, and I had even less reason to believe her now. I suspected that she had found that Bible and had begun reading it, triggering some painful feelings, but not the exact memories. The painful feelings could be the triggering mechanism for engaging a different personality—just as they had been when she was a child. Then it occurred to me that if she did indeed have more than one personality, her nightclub cruising behavior might have come from one of her ''other'' personalities. As I thought more and more about it, the possibility of more than one personality explained a lot. But I was getting ahead of myself. Waiting to see where Jacqueline would take us, I was surprised when toward the end of the next session she abruptly said, ''I've decided to quit therapy for a while. It seems to be doing more harm than good.''

Realizing I didn't have much to lose by pushing her now, I risked responding, ''That's because we're getting close to something you don't want to remember. Your memory will be painful, but it will help you get better—to feel whole again.''

''You're probably right, but I've decided I need a rest for now. I'll get back to it later.''

Her tone didn't leave any room for negotiation, so I thought it wise not to try. However, there was something I needed to be reassured of. ''You've been acting different lately and I need to know whether you're okay. You're not going to do something self-destructive, are you?''

''If you mean am I going to try to kill myself again, the answer is no. I won't do that again. I promise.''

''Well, I'm not ready for you to quit but it's your call, not mine. I just want you know that you can come back any time.''

''I will come back, but not just now.''

When she left I experienced the familiar feeling of frustration that comes from a patient ending therapy before resolution of the conflict that brought him or her there in the first place. It happens from time to time, but I still have to remind myself that people have to handle their pain in their own way. Sometimes running away from it is the best they can do at the time. A good percentage of those who do leave without resolution really do come back at a later time. But with Jacqueline I couldn't tell.

She didn't call back. There were times when I would somehow be reminded of her, and I would momentarily wonder where she was and how she was doing. And there were times when the clinician in me wondered if she truly was a multiple personality. I had come to accept that I would never know the answer to that question when events called that acceptance into question.

I received a call from a man who wanted to set up an appointment with me. He said he was referred to me by a friend of his, a former patient named Jacqueline. The appointment was made, but after hanging up the phone I had a lingering feeling that something wasn't right. It had been almost two years since my last visit with Jacqueline so I retrieved her file and began to review the case. Then it struck me what it was that seemed out of place. Jacqueline had never had any male friends. Perhaps, I thought, her life had changed a lot in two years.

My new patient turned out to be an attractive man in his mid- to late forties. He had gorgeous, penetrating blue eyes that seemed very familiar to me. As we introduced ourselves, I couldn't stop wondering where I had seen this man before.

"Have we met before?" I asked.

"No."

"You look so familiar to me."

"We haven't formally met."

"Formally?"

"Well, several years ago you attended an AA meeting. I was at that meeting. I didn't think you would remember."

Of course, I thought, he was the attractive man whom I spotted that evening. The one all the woman were interested in who wasn't interested in any of them. I wondered if Jacqueline had met him through AA. "You said on the phone you were a friend of Jacqueline's."

"That's right."

He didn't offer any more information and I was reluctant to ask further questions. In my business, confidentiality is sacred, so when a person is referred to me by a former patient, I don't ask many questions about their connection to each another. Instead, I accept whatever information they want to give me. Apparently, this man didn't want to give me much.

"Well, how can I help you?" I asked.

He shifted nervously in his chair, ran a hand through his thick head of wavy blonde hair, took a deep breath, and began, "I've cut myself off from the world. Except when I'm working, I have no social contacts at all. I haven't had a relationship with a woman in years, even on a friendly basis. I can't even remember the last time I had sex. I've felt this way for a long time, yet I do nothing about it."

"Is there something going on in your life right now that makes this feel more distressing?"

"Why do you ask that?"

"You said you've felt this way for a long time, so I'm curious why you're choosing to do something about it now."

He didn't answer at first. Instead, he stared directly at me and gave me a look that made me feel as if I somehow had the answer to my own question. Finally, he simply said, "Jacqueline."

"Jacqueline?"

"I want to have a relationship with Jacqueline."

As soon as he said it, I sensed trouble. "What kind of relationship?" I asked, thinking I'd better clarify before I made any false assumptions.

"Kind?" he asked, as if puzzled by my question.

"Well, you said she was your friend. Do you want more

than a friendship? Do you want a sexual relationship as well?''

''I'm not sure,'' he responded. ''I just know I want to get to know her better—to be more intimate with her.''

''Does Jacqueline know how you feel?''

''I'm not sure . . . she keeps her distance.''

I thought to myself, yes, I bet she does. My next thought had to do with the complexity of what was at hand. A socially isolated man attempting to break out of his isolation by choosing a socially isolated woman whose sexual preference just happens to be for women, not men. It had all the ingredients of a recipe called disaster.

''What about Jacqueline attracts you?'' I asked, hoping to discover why he was choosing such a low-probability situation when he apparently could pick from many women.

''She intrigues me where other women don't.''

''Do you know what it is about her that intrigues you?''

''Not really.''

''Does she remind you of anyone else you've known? Someone from your past perhaps? Someone you especially liked?''

''I hadn't thought about that. I don't know who it could be. I haven't known many women in my life, except for my mother. And it certainly wouldn't be her, that's for sure.''

''Why do you say that?''

''I'm not in the least bit intrigued by my mother. In fact, I don't like my mother and have as little to do with her as possible. She made my life miserable. You see, she wanted a girl. Ever since I could remember I felt as if I didn't belong in this world . . .''

He continued talking, but I was distracted. If I hadn't just looked at Jacqueline's case notes, it might never have struck me that he was repeating her refrain. Then, a strange thought entered my mind. Could it be possible that his attraction to Jacqueline was a result of something as mystical as kindred spirits? Two people who both felt they never belonged in this world certainly had something strong in common. But I didn't want to miss what he was saying, so I forced my attention back to his words.

". . . she kept my hair long and dressed me up in clothing that was more feminine than masculine. My brothers seemed to enjoy making fun of me. In fact, lots of people made fun of me." He paused for a moment and looked away. Then he turned back to me, and I noticed he had moisture in his eyes as he spoke. "My mother seemed oblivious to the cruelty of what she was doing."

"What about your father? How did he react to all this?"

"My father was a drunk. He yelled a lot—at her, at all of us—but he never did anything to really help me out. I vividly remember him in his drunken state yelling at her, 'You're going to turn that kid into a fag,' but she didn't stop, and all he did was to keep yelling that at her. I don't have much respect for my father. Actually, that's too kind. He's a loser."

As I listened to this man, I couldn't keep my thoughts away from the kindred-spirit possibility. He had so much in common with Jacqueline that it seemed preternatural. Jacqueline had brothers who were mean to her and a father who was a drunk. Of course, having an alcoholic parent is not so unusual and neither are cruel siblings. But the common feeling of not belonging told me there was more than just coincidence going on. Unfortunately, our time was over and would have to wait until our next visit to satisfy my curiosity.

All the next day the kindred-spirit idea kept floating in and out of my mind. I vacillated between thinking I was letting my imagination go wild and thinking I had discovered a true mystical happening. Several days later I was still reviewing this in my mind when I received a letter in the mail. The handwriting seemed familiar, but I didn't place it right away. It wasn't until I opened it and discovered a fragile, yellowed page from Genesis that I realized why it seemed familiar.

Now I was really confused. How did Samantha fit in to the picture? I wondered. My new patient hadn't mentioned anything about knowing Samantha. Obviously, she was somehow involved and up to her old tricks. I was beginning to feel like Sherlock Holmes in the midst of a complicated mystery, so I turned to my clue for some answers.

The page was from Genesis 17 and contained three sections: "Circumcision instituted as sign of Abrahamic Covenant," "Promise concerning Isaac, in whom the line of Christ runs," and "Ishmael to be a nation." As before, I knew there was a message I was supposed to get, but after reading the entire page several times, I was as confused as when I started. It was clear that I needed to know my new patient much better before any of what I was reading would make sense. The prudent thing to do was simply to wait until our next session.

I have to admit I was caught up in the mysteriousness of it all and was looking forward to what I would find out in the next visit with my new patient. So it was with some eagerness that I went to the waiting area to greet him. The eagerness turned into astonishment; I was caught totally off guard by what I found.

"You look like you weren't expecting me," Jacqueline said.

"I'm scheduled to see your friend."

"What friend?"

"Your friend Jack."

"Jack?"

"Look, I'm more than a little confused. I'm also a little irritated because I think the three of you are playing some sort of elaborate game with me."

"The *three* of us?"

"Yes; you, Jack, and Samantha."

"Samantha isn't involved in this, and I don't know who this person Jack is."

"Well, then who sent me that page from Genesis?"

"What page from Genesis? I don't know anything about that either."

"I received an envelope in the mail with Samantha's handwriting on it. It contained a page torn out of the Bible."

"Did you save the envelope? I'd like to see the handwriting."

"As a matter of fact, I did." I retrieved the envelope and showed it to her.

"This isn't Samantha's handwriting."

"Are you sure?"

"Yes, I'm quite sure."

"Do you know who wrote this?"

"No."

"Is it Jack's?"

"I told you, I don't know a Jack."

"Jacqueline, I think you're playing with me. I can't help you or Jack if you're not honest with me."

"But I am being honest with you. I'm not sure whose handwriting that is. I just know it isn't Samantha's."

This wasn't getting us anywhere so I invited her into my office and said, "Last week I met with a man named Jack who said he was a friend of yours and that you referred him to me. He was scheduled to be here today."

"That's very strange. I really don't know someone named Jack."

If this was really true, then I was curious as to why Jacqueline would mysteriously reappear after several years. She seemed to believe she had scheduled an appointment. Obviously, one of us was very confused so I asked, "Did you call my office to make an appointment for today?"

Jacqueline looked surprised and then thoughtful, as if trying to recall whether she did. Finally, she answered, "I don't remember doing it. But when I woke up today, I knew I was supposed to be here."

"And you still maintain you don't know anybody named Jack."

"Look, I've told you I don't. Why do you keep asking me about this person? Apparently I've made a mistake about my appointment, and I'm not supposed to be here so I'll just leave." Then she rose from her chair and hurriedly walked from the room.

I started to call to her to come back, but I didn't, probably because I was still irritated at what I suspected was some game the two (or three) of them were playing with me. The decision not to ask her back was a mistake, but, as it turned out, not the only mistake I had made with these cases or, more accurately, with this case.

It was only later that evening, when I was driving home and thinking back on Jacqueline's visit that day, that something she said finally hit home, and I thought I had found the missing piece to this complicated puzzle. She had said, "I woke up this morning and knew I was supposed to be here." It was as if someone else had made the appointment for her, and I now thought I knew who might have done that.

I turned off at the next exit and went back to my office to get both pages from the Bible and to get a particular book I thought would tell me if what I was thinking was a possibility. With excited anticipation, I put the three items in my briefcase and drove home. As soon as I got home, I pulled out the book, *Man & Woman, Boy & Girl* by John Money and Anke Ehrhardt. I flipped to the index and quickly found the subject I was looking for: multiple (dual) personality: transvestism. I felt an uncomfortable excitement as my fingers searched for the indicated page. If what I was thinking was right, I had missed all the clues. And I had missed an opportunity to help a confused individual work through a painful but necessary union.

So it was with mixed emotions that I read the passage:

Transvestism as a form of fetishism in the male is not too far removed from transexualism, a condition which dictates that a person, in the present instance a male, totally and continuously impersonates a female in sexual anatomy as well as clothing and behavior.

. . . and a great many male transvestite impersonators who do not desire a permanent sex reassignment are uncannily expert at metamorphosing from one sex role and mode of dress to another. Even the voice is changed in pitch and loudness. One has here a manifestation akin to the phenomenon of multiple personality, well known in R. L. Stevenson's story of Dr. Jekyll and Mr. Hyde.

On the basis of today's evidence—and here one must be judiciously tentative—it appears that the period of greatest risk for errors of gender-identity formation, of long-lasting effect in the brain, is after birth, and at around the time of acquiring the native language.

What all this meant was that Jacqueline and Jack were one and the same person, a biological male. Easy to see the juxtaposition of the names now that I knew the truth. Apparently, when assuming the role of Jacqueline ''she'' lived in a completely delusionary world—a world passed on from a mother whose desperation for a daughter caused her to deny the true gender of her child.

No wonder his brothers teased him as a child. His mother, treating him as female, confused his developing gender identity, most likely producing effeminate behavior. To feel like he belonged in the world, to be accepted by the mother he adored, *he* had to be a *she*. Jacqueline was loved by her mother and loved her in return. Jack was rejected by his mother and hated her in return. Jack had memories of being humiliated by being dressed in effeminate clothing. But if he became Jacqueline, he could stop the humiliation, so Jacqueline had no memories of humiliation.

In early childhood Jack's gender blurring, although ridiculing, could be passed off in society. Little boys often have long hair and wear cute clothing. But as he grew older, it became increasingly difficult to face the world without taking a side. Then, adolescent male hormones kicked in, challenging his pretense and forcing him to proclaim an either/or identity to society. With social pressure acting on him from the outside to choose his anatomical maleness, and the need to feel loved acting on him from the inside to choose his femaleness, the conflict was torturous. In an attempt to deal with this conflict, Jack came up with a brilliant but ultimately self-defeating solution: He would be both.

He joined the basketball team (a male not a female team as I had originally assumed) and began to live the outside life of a male. But in love relationships, his destiny would be female—because being female was the only way he had ever felt love. And if he could have avoided the issue of his emerging sexuality and remained platonic in his love relationships, it might have been a strained but successful solution.

But imagine how confusing the issue of sex was for this he/she. When approached sexually by his two male teammates, the confusion must have been overwhelming. Especially, if as I suspected, the earlier sexual incidents in the barn with his brother (or brothers) took place. From his biblical teaching, he knew that sex with males was sinful, making enemies of those whose "seed" was eaten in vain. The sexual incidents in the barn most likely consisted of mutual oral sex, which in Jack's mind would have meant that his seed had been eaten in vain. Acknowledging the truth of this meant that Jack was breaking God's covenant, a thought so intolerable to Jack that his mind couldn't accept it. To keep from breaking God's covenant, in all matters of a sexual nature, Jack "became" Jacqueline and, therefore, *not* homosexual.

Cases of this type, although bizarre and rare, are attempts to solve what appears to be an otherwise unsolvable predicament. Although physiologically male, the psychologically female part of Jack is the part that falls in love with the man. To Jack, it's not a homosexual relationship, but to the partner it is. The cross-dressing may, at first, be hidden from the male partner. Eventually, however, the need for Jack to cross-dress and assume the outward appearance of a female becomes essential for sexual arousal to occur. Usually, a certain amount of this behavior is accepted, but if the behavior accelerates, the partner may become alienated.

This is what was happening in the relationships Jacqueline explained to me—all of which were with men, not women as I originally had assumed. As he, Jack, anticipated possible rejection of his cross-dressing from his partner, his need for acceptance grew (just as when he was a child searching for acceptance from his mother). Acceptance had always come from being female, so Jacqueline would increasingly emerge. I can only speculate that this caused further alienation from his partners, which in turn increased Jack's fear of rejection. Destined to "flee when none pursueth you," *she* headed for the clubs and bars, compulsively searching for love and acceptance. But what she ended up with instead was more rejection, and sometimes worse, physical abuse. Failing to find the needed acceptance in the bars, she would retreat for months or years, only to re-create the cycle again at some later point. Clearly, alcohol had been an attempt to deaden the rejection and constant feelings of not belonging. The alcohol had kept the pain at a barely manageable level for thirty years. Without it, however, the need for conflict resolution mounted and Jack chose to seek therapy.

Why was it then that Jacqueline and not Jack originally showed up in my office? My guess is that it was simply easier for Jack to send his alter ego to be "fixed." In that way, he could stay intact and free from blame. This is a common occurrence in therapy: One partner *sends* the other to therapy to get fixed. On closer investigation, it often turns out that the one who is not in therapy has the main problem. Skilled at manipulation, the problematic partner has masterfully convinced the other partner he or she is to blame. In this case, Jacqueline certainly felt she was the despicable character while Jack, the puppeteer, pulled all the strings.

What Jack must have wanted in his unconscious mind was for a merger to take place: Jacqueline was to "meet" Jack. Jack, not Samantha (was there even a Samantha?), had been sending me those biblical clues. He wanted me to know about Jacqueline, but I had not understood about the gender confusion and had missed the opportunity. Originally, that's why Jack quit sending Jacqueline to therapy— his plan of a merger wasn't successful. Then, Jack came back later, hoping that by "showing" himself to me, I would make the connection.

That's why Jack had sent me the passage from Genesis mentioning male circumcision. Wanting a girl, it was unlikely his mother had had Jack circumcised. I looked at the page from Genesis and there it was: *And the uncircumcised male child whose flesh of his foreskin is not circumcised, that soul shall be cut off from his people; he had broken my covenant.* To Jack, it must have seemed as if his soul had been cut off from his people. Not only had he been shamed by his biological anatomy, but he had once again broken God's law by not being circumcised. By sending me the page from Genesis, he had been trying to get me to understand that Jacqueline had been born a male. Then, on the next visit he showed up as Jacqueline. Surely, I would get his message now. But once again I missed the clues. Feeling hopeless and rejected—the one emotion that she/he couldn't handle—Jacqueline walked out of my office.

Perhaps, I thought, it wasn't too late to make amends. I would call Jack tomorrow and ask him if he would be willing to return. I looked at his chart the next day and found that he had given me only a home phone. Curious, I went to Jacqueline's chart to see what she had listed. There was no work phone. That would make sense because it was Jack, not Jacqueline, who was in the insurance business and

Jacqueline would never have wanted me to call her at the office. There was a home phone number listed for Jacqueline, however. As I suspected, the number was the same as Jack's. I waited until that evening to call, only to receive one more surprise when an unfamiliar voice said hello. I had been counting on recognizing the voice so I would know whether I was talking to Jack or Jacqueline. Could this be Samantha? I wondered. It was hard to tell if the voice was male or female. A couple of years ago I had assumed it was female, but perhaps Samantha was really a Sam. In this confusing situation, it could certainly be possible.

I decided to take my best guess on whom to ask for: "Is Jack there?"

"Who is this?" the voice demanded.

I identified myself and waited to see what would happen.

"Well, you certainly screwed things up, didn't you?"

"Is this Sam?" I ventured.

"Yes."

"I guess you remember me."

"What I remember is that you didn't want to listen to me."

"I'm sorry about that, but it seemed the right thing at the time. "I'm looking for Jack. Can you help me?"

"Jack's not here."

"Is Jacqueline there?" I risked. I could be revealing a secret, but I didn't know any other way around it.

"Jack's gone. He moved out today."

"Do you know where I can reach him?"

"No, he wouldn't tell me where he was going."

"Do you have his number at work?"

There were a few moments of silence at the other end of the phone, followed by a big sigh and then the number. I felt relief as I hung up the phone. It had been a difficult call for both of us.

I called Jack's office the next day but was told that Jack would be out of the office for a few days. I left a message for him to call me. A week went by and he didn't return my call. I tried reaching him again and this time was told that Jack had transferred to another office in another state. I suspected he must have told the receptionist not to put my calls through because I called his new office several times and could never reach him. I left messages, but he never returned my calls.

Finally, I had to accept the fact that I had missed the brief window of opportunity to make the most important introduction of my life.

DARLENE

No Trespassing

Meet Darlene, the kind of person you instantly take a liking to. She's upbeat, refreshingly honest, and has a friendly smile. Like an excited child, she has a tendency to talk quickly, making it easy to get caught up in her enthusiasm. She also radiates a natural sensual energy, most notably in the clothing she chooses to cover her shapely body. Tasteful, but definitely sexy, her style of dress and the way she handles her body give the impression that she is comfortable with her sexuality. Nothing could be further from the truth: Darlene is phobic about sex. At thirty-eight and married for nine years, Darlene has been unable to consummate her marriage.

Darlene has a condition known as *vaginismus*. With any attempt at penetration, the muscles surrounding her vagina involuntarily tighten, making penetration impossible. The cause of vaginismus is not physiological. Its origin is psychological; a response similar in many ways to phobias such as fear of heights, snakes, or flying. The anticipation of dealing with the feared situation or object creates an anxiety that causes physical changes in the body such as heart palpitations, sweating, dizziness, or immobilization. A person who is afraid of heights, for example, may find that his body actually freezes upon finding himself in a feared situation. In Darlene's case, her body automatically responds to the fear of penetration by constricting the vaginal muscles.

Like many phobias, Darlene's vaginismus was a conditioned response. That is, it was a learned behavior resulting from the association of an unpleasant feeling or sensation with the event that originally caused the unpleasant feeling. For example, *agoraphobia*, the most common of all phobic disorders, is the fear of being alone in a public place from which the person thinks escape would be difficult or help unavailable if he or she were incapacitated. Often, the first time a person may have had this feeling was as a child separated from a parent in a store or amusement park. For some children, the fear of being abandoned never goes away completely, lurking instead in the unconscious long after the child is reunited with the parent. In adulthood, situations that resemble the original one can re-create the fear, resulting in a phobic reaction. Thus, being in an overly crowded place triggers the recall of the original feelings of terror at being abandoned. Not all phobic reactions, however, have their origins in childhood. A terrifying car accident as an adult may be enough to create a phobia about driving.

Vaginismus is not common. Over the years, I have treated fewer than half a dozen cases, but Darlene's was by far the worst case I'd ever encountered. At the mere mention of the world "intercourse," she would begin to exhibit signs of anxiety. Her body would become restless, her breathing rapid, she would grip the sides of the chair, and make facial expressions one would expect from someone being tortured. Change the subject and Darlene would become the charming, endearing, delightful person of the previous moment. This is exactly what happened on the very first day I met her.

Upon entering my office, she immediately became a nervous wreck. She had made a promise to herself to tell me her problem in the beginning of the session and was obviously struggling with her decision. Like a caged animal determined to be free from captivity, Darlene pushed herself to say aloud the words that created the images she so feared.

"I've been anxious ever since I made this appointment. This morning I thought I'd never make it through the day. I almost turned my car around three times on the way here. I'm so embarrassed about my problem, but after all these years, I think now I'm really ready to face it. You'll have to excuse me for talking so fast, but I just have to get the words out before my courage leaves me. You see, my husband and I have been married nine years but we've never had intercourse. We do other things, of course, but if he even puts his penis near my vagina . . . well, I freak out."

Her hands had gripped the arms of the chair, and her face had become contorted when she said the words "penis near my vagina," but after having spoken, her facial expression returned to normal and then assumed a look similar to that of a child pleased with herself. Then she fumbled around in her purse, finally drawing out a letter which she handed to me at the same time that she said, "I want to go to this."

It was a letter from a reunion committee announcing a twentieth high-school reunion. The letter was requesting information on "lost" names and addresses. I noticed that the date of the reunion was still almost a year away.

"There's a connection between your visit here and this reunion?" I asked.

"Very definitely. If you look you'll see that the letter is signed by a man named Harold?"

"Yes . . ."

"Well, Harold's one reason I'm here. I haven't been able to face Harold in fifteen years, and I want to be able to walk up to him and talk to him as if he was just another person."

"You say Harold's one reason you're here."

"Harold's the only man I've ever had sexual intercourse with. It was only once, fourteen years ago. June 16th to be exact. Obviously, I've never forgotten the experience." As she was speaking, her body once again became tense, and her face momentarily assumed the same frightened, almost tortured, look that I was to see again and again over the next year.

Darlene spent the rest of the session explaining to me about Harold. He was her first love. They were only fifteen when they started hanging around together, and soon they were going steady. Harold had great promise as a star football player, and all the girls were jealous of Darlene's ability to get such a "catch." Darlene claimed to remember the euphoric feelings "as if it were yesterday," not twenty-three years ago. She readily gave her heart to Harold, but she wouldn't give him her body. Her mother had warned her many times that girls who gave in to the sexual urges of boys were nothing but tramps, and Darlene didn't want to be something as awful as a tramp.

Harold put a lot of pressure on Darlene to go all the way with him. He had even pleaded with her that "if you really love me, you'll do this for me." It tore her up to see Harold so frustrated, but she was just too afraid of going all the way. In the beginning of their relationship they fought a lot about it but somehow always managed to make up. Then, Darlene heard a rumor that Harold was "doing it" with another girl, a girl who had a reputation as a tramp. Just the thought that he might betray her this way caused a terrible pain in her heart. She worried about it for days and was unable to sleep because of dreams of being trampled on by an army of soldiers. Finally, she had to know the truth; not knowing was turning her into a wreck. So, she confronted him with the rumor. He denied it but then angrily told her he thought he "had a right to get it where he could if she wasn't willing to put out."

His words stung so sharply that the ache in her heart began to feel more like a huge crack. Darlene didn't want to lose Harold, but she just couldn't do what he asked. Immediately afterward Darlene was sorry she had reacted so strongly. Harold was the most important thing in her life. Without him she felt incomplete and unable to function. She considered calling him and telling him she was sorry, but before she got up the courage, a girlfriend told her she had seen Harold with the girl with the bad reputation. When Darlene asked where she had seen them, her girlfriend was reluctant to answer. Darlene begged, finally getting her friend to tell her she had seen them at a party getting "hot and heavy." When Darlene heard this, she knew there would be no phone call to Harold. It was over between them.

It took weeks for Darlene to be able to get through an entire day without crying. And to make it even more difficult, she had to hide her unhappiness from her mother. Her mother had hated Harold from the beginning, but then her mother seemed to hate all boys. She certainly didn't want to give her mother the satisfaction of knowing that Harold had hurt her badly. Her mother would only say "I told you so."

Several months after their breakup, Darlene was able to have what you might call a normal day. For her, that meant she didn't well up with tears and feel as if someone was directly shooting poison into her heart. But every time she saw Harold, her heart would skip a beat and she would be flooded with unpleasant longing to have him back. Harold, on the other hand, didn't seem at all disturbed by their breakup. He had many girlfriends after Darlene. In fact, Darlene eventually lost count of all the girls who claimed to have been Harold's girl. She, on the other hand, didn't have any more boyfriends in high school because she felt convinced the same thing would happen: He'd want sex, she'd say no, she'd get dumped. It simply wasn't worth the heartache.

After high school, Harold went away to college, which greatly relieved Darlene. She wouldn't have to see him parading around with a different girl all the time. Out of sight, out of mind, she hoped. Anyway, she had more important things to do than think about boys. Boys had one-track minds and didn't like being denied. She was going to do something with her life so she wouldn't be dependent on a man. Men seemed interested in only one thing.

As I listened to Darlene, I realized she had developed a defense mechanism common to those with feelings of rejection that come from unrequited love. It's a form of "sour grapes" in which the person convinces herself she no longer desires that which has caused her so much pain. Instead, she sublimates her desire into other interests, work being the most common.

Darlene had made a promise to herself that she would never again let a man hurt her the way Harold had. Yet here she was, still talking about Harold more than twenty years later. Whatever had intervened in those years was sure to be significant and, most likely, out of the ordinary.

I brought my attention back to her story. She was telling me how she had attended a local junior college as a business major and, when she finished, had started working in a bank. She went out with men occasionally, but only as friends. Getting involved with a man meant sex would, sooner or later, become an issue between them. It did not escape Darlene, however, that men paid attention to her. She knew she had a sexy body and had been taught to believe that, being prisoners of their sexual desires, men couldn't help but notice women's bodies. She prided herself on the notion that unlike other women, she simply didn't care about being the object of their obsessive desires.

She was glad to be involved in her career and free of guys like Harold. Then all of that changed by a freak coincidence.

She had been working in the same bank for three years and had moved up from being a teller to a position in new accounts. When her supervisor left to go to another bank, Darlene hoped that she would be promoted. So she was disappointed to learn that a new supervisor was being hired. She was astounded when she found out the new supervisor would be Harold. At the moment she heard his name, her heart skipped a beat and she felt faint. She just didn't think she could work in the same place with the man who had practically ruined her life.

He was due to start in one week, and every day prior to his arrival on the job, she thought about quitting. The whole thing seemed so unfair. Her life was on a path she had carefully and meticulously created. A path that didn't include men. How was it possible that of all the banks in the city, Harold was ending up in hers? But as unfair as it seemed, she realized that quitting would just be allowing him to continue to control her life. Anyway, it had been five years since she had seen him. Most likely, she was completely over him and he wouldn't affect her that much.

However, the day Harold showed up for work was the most nerve-racking day of her life. In spite of her resolve to be strong, she couldn't keep her mind from wondering what it would be like when they were face to face. Would he even remember her? Would he ignore her? Would he make some snide remark? And what would she do? She was so nervous she thought she might faint right on the spot. But none of these things happened. Harold was very pleasant to her and even told her she looked marvelous and that it would be nice to have an old pal around.

The last comment stunned Darlene. Old pal? Obviously, he had forgotten how much he had hurt her. Well, two can play this game, she thought. She'd show him that he didn't mean anything to her. But playing the game was more stressful than she counted on. She didn't know why he affected her the way he did, but she felt the same feelings toward him that she had back in high school. Just being around him made her heart race and her face blush. And she was always trying to please him—just as she had as a teenager. Getting dressed for work now became an ordeal. Nothing in her closet seemed right. Her wardrobe needed a definite face-lift. How was it possible that she hadn't noticed before how childish her clothes were? She was a woman now, and she needed to dress in a more sophisticated fashion. She worried only momentarily what a new wardrobe would do to her bank account. After all, what were credit cards for?

She spent more money than she had ever imagined she could spend on clothes, but it paid off. She received continual compliments from her co-workers. The compliments caused Darlene to do something she had never done before—take a closer look at her body. She knew she was sexy, but not once had she ever *really* looked at herself nude in the mirror. When she gave it a try, she felt terribly uncomfortable. The more she thought about it, the more she realized that her Victorian mother had shamed her into avoiding all matters of bodily function. Painfully, she had to admit that she had emerged into womanhood as a prude. And, worse, she had justified her prudishness by deciding *all* men were sex fiends. If nothing else, she thought, Harold's reappearance on the scene had brought her into the twentieth century. Without having a specific plan in mind, Darlene committed herself to shedding her puritanical background.

She couldn't say exactly what it was that she did differently besides change her style of dress, but, whatever it was, it seemed to work. The men in the office were definitely friendlier and more flirtatious with her, especially Harold. It was a confusing time for Darlene. Admiration from men felt good, not degrading, as her mother had repeatedly drilled into her head.

As the weeks passed and Darlene let the changes in her

life sink in, a new and powerful emotion came to her awareness: anger at her mother. If her mother hadn't been so unbearably negative about sex, she might never have lost Harold in the first place. A vision came to her. She would have a second chance with Harold, and this time she wouldn't hold back.

It was surprisingly easy to get Harold to ask her out for a date. She was nervous the entire time, but she felt she did a great job of covering it up. He was as charming as ever and he was polite. She was thankful he didn't make any sexual advances because she needed more time to get up her courage. He asked her out again and this time he made an approach. As she felt Harold's passion mount, Darlene's courage failed her and she kept Harold at bay. Harold became frustrated and sarcastically commented that she hadn't changed much in five years. Darlene protested that she had changed, but she just needed a little time.

They had a third date and Darlene knew it was now or never. If she was to keep Harold in her life, she would have to let go of her virginity. Recently, she had grown to hate her virginity and had told herself she was ready to discard it. So when Harold became passionate as expected, Darlene talked to herself, telling herself to relax. She reminded herself she was doing this because it was what she wanted. When she didn't resist, Harold, like a wild man, was all over her, touching her breasts and putting his hand between her legs. Now that it was happening to her, she realized it wasn't how she had imagined it would be. She thought she would love his kisses, but instead, he covered her mouth with his and pushed his tongue into her so hard that she couldn't breathe.

And he kept pushing his pelvis at her, grinding the bulge between her legs on her thigh. He pressed so hard he was hurting her. His movements seemed desperate and out of control, as if he was being driven by some sort of demon. She wanted to scream out for him to get off her, but she knew she couldn't stop. Harold would never see her again if she backed out now. So, she let Harold have his way. In no time at all he had her sweater up around her neck, her bra undone, and her panties off. His hands were all over her and seemed everywhere at once. Somehow he had managed to get his own pants down.

Darlene was stunned into motionlessness, but Harold didn't even seem to notice. She knew she had made a mistake but also knew it was too late to do anything about it. All she could think about was wishing it was over. Then, without warning, it happened. He was pushing his penis inside her and he was making these horrible grunting noises. She felt pain, fear, and then obliteration. Harold was so involved with his own pleasure he didn't even notice that Darlene was practically in a state of panic. He was repeatedly thrusting his body at her, and he had his mouth on top of hers' so she could hardly breathe. The pain Darlene felt inside her was blurred only by the fact that she thought she was suffocating.

Then he let out a cry and his body shuddered. All Darlene could think about was that the thrusting pain inside her had finally stopped. It was over now, she thought, and he would get off of her and let her breathe. But he didn't move from on top of her, and his body felt like dead weight, crushing her beneath him. She wanted him off and she wanted air. She had found it difficult to breathe while Harold was inside of her, but now she felt as if she would die from lack of air. She wanted to scream but couldn't find the strength or the air. In her mind she saw the familiar image of hundreds of soldiers, only this time they were trampling across her chest and wouldn't let her breathe. Just as she was sure she would black out, Harold grunted and rolled off of her.

He lay next to her in what seemed almost an unconscious state, breathing hard, but not as hard as Darlene. It seemed like an eternity before she felt air moving freely in and out of her lungs. She just wanted to lie there and breathe, but her attention kept being drawn to a terrible pain inside her and something slimy and sticky between her legs. She moved her body a little bit and the pain intensified. She felt a panic start to build again because she knew she was supposed to do something about the mess. But all she wanted to do was die. It hadn't been anything like what she had read about or seen in the movies. She felt cheated, angry, and scared.

It was the need to clean up the mess she felt between her legs that finally made her crawl out of the bed. As she stood up she felt the blood rush from her head and she thought she would faint. She sat back down for a moment and let the feeling pass. Then she headed for the bathroom and was immediately reminded not only of the pain, but that the warm stickiness was now dripping down her legs. She quickened her pace, afraid to mess up the carpet. Once she was inside the bathroom she looked down at her body and started to cry. She had expected a little blood, but when she actually saw it, fear gripped her body, immediately followed by a feeling of shame. She didn't know why she felt such panic, only that she didn't want Harold to see her so distraught. She decided to take a shower, thinking it would help her feel clean and that then she could face Harold. But no matter how much she washed between her legs, she couldn't get rid of the feeling that she was dirty. She kept turning the water hotter and hotter, somehow believing the hotter the water, the more she could wash away the pain, the fear, and the unrelenting shame. She wanted to stay in the shower forever, but the thought that Harold might get tired of waiting and just leave forced her to turn off the water.

She put on a robe and came out of the bathroom to face Harold. He was partially dressed and had pulled the sheets off the bed, rolled them up in a ball, and thrown them in the corner. Looking at the sheets caused Darlene to feel the same panic she had felt earlier in the bathroom. Surely he would be disgusted with her for making such a mess, she thought. She found she couldn't look him in the eyes and, instead, stood there like a criminal being sentenced, her head hanging down. She knew he was staring at her and that she was expected to do something, but she felt immobilized. Then she became aware that he was searching for the remainder of his clothes, and again the panic heightened. He was going to leave her and she would never see him again. She forced herself to look at him, but he was now busy buttoning up his shirt. When he finished he looked at her and said, "I thought you said you had changed."

Inside Darlene was trembling yet hoping that Harold couldn't see how shaken she was. She certainly didn't want to lose him after all she had been through, so she said what she thought he wanted to hear. "I wanted you to be the first."

"Don't do my any favors," he replied as he bent over to pick up his shoes. He sat down on the unmade bed and put them on. Then he looked up at Darlene but remained silent. Finally, he walked over to her, held her in his arms, and said, "I'm sorry, that was a mean thing to say." He kissed her on the forehead and whispered in her ear, "I've got to be going. I'll see you on Monday morning."

Darlene stood frozen in place as she watched him leave the bedroom and then heard the front door close. She slowly shuffled over to the bed and lay down on it, knowing she didn't have the strength to make up a new bed. There was a small blood stain on her mattress which caused her to have a sick feeling—a permanent reminder of this horrible evening, she thought. Totally exhausted but unable to sleep, she lay in a fetal position on the bed, going over and over the events of the evening. What a stupid fool she was to let Harold be the first. She should have known better. But then nobody had prepared her to feel pain or to deal with the mess. And the fear had seemed to come out of nowhere. Maybe she was overreacting. After all, he had apologized to her. She finally fell asleep, having convinced herself that everything would be fine on Monday—just as Harold had said.

Monday morning came and Darlene was once again a nervous wreck. So when Harold was friendly to her, she felt a great sense of relief. Several days went by, however, and he didn't say anything to her about going out. Then the invitation for their fifth high-school reunion came in the mail. She had been expecting it—after all, Harold was chairman of the reunion committee and had been talking about it. She had been looking forward to it, expecting that she and Harold would go together. She had wanted this more than anything. There was something sweet in the irony that she would have him on her arm and together they would face his former flame.

More days went by and Harold said nothing about any further dates, including the reunion. Darlene was beginning to panic. Could her worst fear come true after all? Would he jilt her again? The weekend came and went without a word from Harold. Darlene spent the whole weekend in tears. Had her mother been right after all? Did sex degrade a woman in a man's eyes? If that was true, how come men like Harold always wanted it so badly? Darlene was both frightened and confused. She had thought losing her virginity would mean gaining Harold, but now it seemed the other way around.

By Monday morning Darlene had convinced herself that she had once again lost Harold. She knew she shouldn't have been surprised when she found out he was taking someone else to the reunion, but giving up her fantasy was more than her logical mind could handle. The thought of him being with someone other than herself was so unbearable, she decided not to go. It had only been important to go because she would have been with him. So, the night of the reunion she stayed home and faced what turned out to be only one of many heartbreaking evenings.

For two agonizing years, Darlene went to work each day, worked side by side with Harold, and lived a charade, pretending she could handle it all. There was much gossip among the women about Harold's good looks and charm and about whom Harold dated. Darlene had let it be known that she couldn't care less about Harold, so she was included in much of the gossip. The truth was that for the first six months since that terrible evening, she drove home each day with tears streaming down her face. The nights were practically unbearable, and Darlene wasn't sure how she made it through them. The next morning, however, she would be back at work, acting a part. She was determined that Harold would not know that he had practically destroyed her, again. And she would not be the one to leave the bank, either. No matter how much it hurt, Harold would not drive her away. To this end she had a victory of sorts. Harold left in order to take a higher-level position in another bank, and Darlene was promoted to his job as supervisor.

Darlene had been telling me her story in rapid fashion, occasionally looking at the clock to be sure she didn't run out of time. She took one final look at the clock and said, "So, I haven't seen him since the day he left to go to another job. When I first got married, I thought I would get over my sexual hang-ups and that I could go to our tenth reunion and face him squarely with my head up high. But marriage didn't solve my sexual problems.

"I know our time is just about up, but I have to know if you think you can help me. I'm tired of running away from my sexual problems, and I feel if I can face Harold, then I can face my sexual problems. They're one and the same to me."

"It's you, not Harold, that you have to face, Darlene. And besides, a time frame is a double-edged sword. It works in your favor because it motivates you to conquer your problem. But it also works against you because it puts pressure on you. You need to take as much time as you need to clear up your problem. Patience will be important."

"Patience is what I think my husband will run out of any day. It's been nine years and I've never been able to let him

penetrate me. I love him and don't want to lose him because of an overblown reaction to some man in my past.
So, do you think you can help me?''

''Yes, but I can't promise it will be in the time frame you
have in your mind, and it probably won't be in the way
you think.''

''Well, as long as I solve this problem, I don't care how
it gets done. But I would like to get started. Now that I'm
finally facing this, I want to get things moving.''

''I'd like to meet with your husband. Do you think he'd
come for an appointment?''

''Are you kidding? He's been after me to get therapy for
years. He's thrilled that I made this appointment. I'll have
him call you.''

Our entire first session had consisted of Darlene's story
about Harold while Jake, her husband, had received only
honorable mention. It's natural to wonder what kind of
person would tolerate nine years of an unconsummated
marriage. It's not unusual in unconsummated marriages of
any duration for both partners to have sexual problems. At
first glance it might seem unlikely that a dysfunctional person would choose another dysfunctional person. But if you
think about it for a moment, you begin to see the conve-
nience of it. What better way *not* to deal with your problem
than by finding someone who has a similar problem.

What's happening in this situation is that the couple silently colludes to avoid dealing with the problem. Months,
then years, go by and the problem is simply not discussed.
The longer it goes unacknowledged between the couple,
the easier it becomes to continue the pretense. To an outsider who doesn't share the problem, it seems impossible
that something this glaring could simply be ignored. One
thing it demonstrates, however, is just how difficult it is to
face a sexual problem in a society that places great emphasis

on sexual prowess but simultaneously has no acceptable outlets for those who fall short of the standard.

Ignorance, inexperience, and inhibition are the three main reasons for lack of consummation. With some women there may be an aversion to sex, ranging from mild to severe, vaginismus being the extreme. The aversion can be the result of sexual molestation or rape. However, aversion to sex is not always created by a traumatic experience or series of experiences. Many times, subtle negative messages are passed from a parent or parents to the child. Passing comments, if frequent enough, about things seen on television or in public, for example, set the stage for negative attitudes. Even the way parents deal with each other regarding issues of affection contributes to the sexual attitudes children develop. Lack of affection in front of children conveys a message that parents are uncomfortable with their sexual feelings. Conversely, parents who are frankly sexual in front of children also set the stage for future problems. Children thrive best in an environment that takes into account their developmental readiness. Exposing children prematurely to explicit adult sexual behavior is overpowering and threatening and may cause a child to associate fear with sexuality.

Males as well as females can develop aversions to sex When a man has an aversion to sex, it is usually accompanied by a dysfunction, such as impotency, premature ejaculation, or an inability to orgasm. Although it occurs less frequently than with females, male children are molested, which can also result in an aversion to sex.

It was with these thoughts in mind that I first met Jake, who turned out to fit none of the above descriptions. Jake *was not* sexually ignorant, inhibited, or inexperienced. And he was not currently sexually dysfunctional. He *was* very much in love with Darlene and very devoted to her. When they met ten years ago, Jake, who was British, had been in the country only a few years. Darlene, then a bank vice-president, had met Jake as a result of arranging a line of credit for his company at her bank. Darlene had been a hard sell, repeatedly turning down Jake's invitations for a date. But Jake had been both patient and persistent, qualities that eventually got around Darlene's tendency to mistrust.

Jake was an import-export dealer who appeared to have a great future. Unfortunately, his maturity had not matched his rapid success. Life in the fast lane had led Jake to the use of recreational drugs and to an eventual addiction to cocaine. For years he had managed to keep his habit under control and hidden from his business associates. He was so good at deception that Darlene was unaware of his habit when she agreed to his marriage proposal.

One of the reasons Darlene had continued to date Jake was that he never pushed her for sex. She was both surprised and relieved to discover this. It never occurred to her that Jake might have a sexual problem himself. And since she didn't know about his cocaine use, she drew no conclusions from that. Jake, however, knew that his addiction was affecting not only his ability to perform but his sexual desire as well. Secretly, he was glad Darlene wasn't pushing him sexually. She seemed to be content to let the issue alone, relieving Jake of embarrassing failures. They married without ever once having attempted intercourse. After the wedding, Jake did make a sexual overture toward Darlene but was unable to maintain his erection. He passed it off to Darlene as being the result of the champagne he had drunk. As always, Darlene was relieved and remained silent.

Over time, Darlene did begin to wonder why Jake was continually having trouble with erections, but relief always won out over curiosity, and it was never discussed. Jake introduced Darlene to oral sex, and it became an important part of their lovemaking. Grateful that she wasn't being asked to have intercourse, Darlene did whatever Jake asked of her. She felt entitled to little pleasure for herself and ended up servicing Jake most of the time without complaint.

But as is frequently the case, Jake's cocaine use slowly

escalated, making it more and more difficult for him to stay underground. Darlene wanted so badly to believe that his late nights, red eyes, and sluggish manner were the result of being overworked, as he claimed. But when the late nights became all-nighters, she could no longer fool herself. Jake's previously perfected social charm began to disintegrate, leaving in its wake frequent embarrassments. Now painfully aware that her husband had a cocaine problem, Darlene tried to beg off from many mandatory social functions. But Jake was still in denial and stubbornly insisting he could handle himself, in spite of repeated disasters. It got so bad that his long-term friend and business partner called Darlene, asking her if she could influence him to seek treatment. No matter how much she pleaded with him to get help, Jake continued to deny that he was out of control.

At parties he would flagrantly flirt with women and then loudly make comments to Darlene about various parts of their bodies. What brought it all crashing down around him was an event intended to bring about a confrontation. Knowing full well that Jake would notice, his business partners failed to invite him to an important social engagement. When he confronted his partners about it, they were brutally honest. "We can't afford to have you there," they said. "You're an embarrassment to us, and worse, you're costing us business. Either get treatment for your addiction, or you're out of here."

Jake continued to deny the truth, preferring instead to curse his long-term friends. Even months after being forced out of the business, he was still insisting he didn't have a problem. Then one night, about three years after their marriage, when Jake was out making a desperate buy, he was picked up by the police and ended up in the county jail. It was at this point that Darlene made the toughest decision of her life. She refused to bail him out.

When the withdrawal symptoms started, Jake was placed in a detox unit. The experience was more agonizing than Jake could have imagined. At first, Darlene's daily visits inflamed him, and he would hurl accusation after accusation at her. On the advice of the counselors, Darlene persisted in her support efforts, waiting for the promised breakthrough. It paid off. Jake did come through the difficult period, and his life started to turn around. The next few months were anything but smooth sailing, but compared to the storm they had just been through, it seemed manageable.

It was a full year before Jake was back in front of his partners asking for another chance and feeling grateful that friendship prevailed. Life without the benefit of an easy high was a difficult transition for him to make. Now that he was without the deceptive bliss of denial, he had to face himself. He had learned in his treatment just how seductive it was to avoid taking responsibility for life's challenges by chemically inducing a feeling of invincible euphoria. Giving up this fantasy was the most difficult part of his recovery and something he knew would be a lifelong effort.

"What I've learned from all of this," he told me, "is that life's just not that simple. I mean, most guys would think I'm crazy to have stayed nine years in a marriage where I wasn't putting it in her. The real truth is that when I was on coke, I wasn't much of a lover myself. I knew Darlene had a problem, but I was too selfish back then to care. She felt so inadequate she didn't dare refuse me. It makes me shudder to think about all the times I took advantage of how insecure she felt about our sex life.

"So, like I said, life isn't that simple. I owe Darlene. I treated her terribly during my coke days, yet she supported me every step of the way, including financially. During the year I was out of work, she paid all the bills. And I don't think I have to tell you what kind of debts an addict can run up.

"I'm not saying I don't have limits. Sometimes I get so frustrated with her, I think about leaving. Then I remind myself of what she did for me and I calm down. But denial is denial, whether it's a drug problem or a sexual problem, and I've learned from my own experience how easy it is for a partner to allow that denial to continue. I'm going to support Darlene in this as long as I see she's making a sincere effort. But I'm not willing any longer to do nothing to change the situation.''

Jake told me that Darlene became a completely different person during sex if he tried to please her in any way. As long as she was doing something for him, she remained calm. But most of the time, if he tried to arouse her by caressing her body, she would stiffen up and make her body completely rigid. Only on rare occasions would she relax and let him please her.

Jake also knew the entire story about Harold but had difficulty believing that the one experience could create the kind of fear he saw on Darlene's face should he put his penis anywhere near her vagina. ''You'd think someone was pointing a gun at her head,'' he said.

''We tried going to a physician sex therapist before, but the man wanted to do a pelvic exam on Darlene. She got as far as putting her legs in the stirrups, but the minute he touched her vagina with that instrument, the same look of fear crossed her face, and she practically kicked him getting off that table.''

I was glad to have this information because it further convinced me that resolution of Darlene's situation would take time. Forcing her to face her phobia had not worked. In fact, it had caused such a negative reaction that it had been three years since Darlene had considered seeking treatment again.

I told Jake that it would take time for Darlene to get over her phobiclike reaction and that his continued patience was necessary.

''I don't see a problem with that,'' he replied. ''As long as she's willing to make an effort. Ever since the day Darlene got that letter in the mail about the reunion, she's the one that's been pushing to do something about solving the problem. It's obviously very important for her to be able to face Harold with dignity. I, on the other hand, just want to punch his face out. Of course, I wouldn't do that because it would deprive Darlene of her satisfaction."

"It's not all good that Darlene has a time frame in mind. It could easily backfire by putting unnecessary pressure on her."

"Maybe so, but I'd be lying if I didn't say I'm glad something's finally motivating her."

Darlene and I had several more history-taking sessions, which allowed me to get the total picture. I wasn't surprised to learn that there were other factors that made her particularly vulnerable to developing a phobiclike reaction to intercourse. Of particular importance were two related events in her life: the start of her menstrual period and the fact that her older sister had become pregnant at age seventeen. Darlene was only thirteen at the time of her sister's pregnancy, but the memory of her mother's reaction was as vivid as if it was yesterday.

When I found out from Darlene that "tramp" was a word her mother often used to describe certain girls, I understood the symbolism of the dreams and images she had of soldiers (men) "tramping" on her. At first, Darlene hadn't understood exactly what her mother meant by the word "tramp." But she didn't have to know exactly what the word meant to understand that it was disgusting. As best as Darlene could tell, the word referred to girls who wore makeup and hung around with boys. Since Darlene thought her older sister Justine was the smartest person alive, she decided one day to ask her what it really meant. So at the ripe old age of eleven, she mustered the courage to ask her fifteen-year-old sister what it really meant.

"Tramps are girls who do it with boys," Justine had replied.

"Do what with boys?" Darlene insisted.

"You know, have sex."

"What is sex anyway?"

"Don't you know anything, dummy? Sex is when the boy puts his penis inside you."

Darlene didn't like it when her sister called her a dummy, so she didn't dare ask any more questions. But she wasn't clear on how or exactly where a penis went inside a girl. She thought about the film she had seen in school about how girls have periods, but she really didn't understand what it had all meant. She vaguely knew periods had something to do with having babies and having babies had something to do with penises. It all seemed so confusing to her she decided to forget about it. Asking her mother was out of the question. Matters of sex disgusted her mother, and she was sure a question about a penis would get the same negative reaction. Now asking her sister was out of the question as well.

Then, when she was thirteen, an emotional tornado hit the family home. There was lots of yelling between Justine and her mother, and both of them did lots of crying as well. Darlene heard only bits and pieces of what was being said, but what she knew for sure was that it had something to do with her mother thinking Justine was a tramp. So Darlene figured that Justine must have been doing it with boys. For several months the tension in the household was unbearable and the fights between Justine and her mother unrelenting.

Then, without warning, the tornado left as quickly as it came—and with it went Justine. Darlene had come home one day to find Justine's things gone from the room. She didn't dare ask her mother what had happened because she knew better than to bring up Justine's name in front of her mother. It was very strange, though, that both her mother and father acted as if nothing at all had happened.

A month or so after Justine's disappearance, Darlene woke up during the night with a pain in her stomach and something wet between her legs. At first she thought she might have somehow wet the bed. Embarrassed, she went into the bathroom to check things out and was horrified to find that something red had ruined her underpants and pajamas. She must be getting her period, she thought. The girls at school had mentioned this from time to time, but Darlene had preferred to think it wouldn't happen to her. In her childish mind, if she never had a period she wouldn't have to worry about being a tramp. Now what was she going to do? She tried washing out the stains in her panties and pajamas, and when she couldn't get them all out, she threw them in the trash. Then she changed underpants and pajamas and stuffed some tissue in her underpants, hoping that would be enough and wishing it would all go away. She went back to bed, but the cramping pain in her stomach kept reminding her that she couldn't wish this thing away. Besides, she had to get up several times to change the tissue because she was afraid she would ruin another pair of panties.

When the morning came she was faced with another dilemma. She couldn't go to school with tissue stuffed in her panties. But if she stayed home, her mother would surely force her to tell her what had happened. She lay there not knowing what to do, and before she knew it her mother was standing in the doorway asking her why she wasn't getting ready for school.

''I don't feel good,'' Darlene said and immediately wished she hadn't.

''What's the matter?'' her mother asked.

''I have a stomachache.''

With these words, her mother took a step inside the room and instinctively Darlene knew she was in for trouble. ''What kind of stomachache?'' her mother asked with a familiar demanding tone in her voice. It was a voice that made Darlene very nervous.

''Just a stomachache.''

''Let me see,'' her mother said and walked over to the bed, reaching for the covers.

Reflexively, Darlene held the covers down. In the dark of the night she hadn't thought about blood on the sheets, but now that it was light, she was sure she must have messed them up too.

"What's going on here, Darlene? What are you hiding?

"Nothing. I'm not hiding anything."

"Then why don't you let me look at your stomach?"

"There's nothing to look at."

"Stop it this minute, Darlene. I'm going to have a look at your stomach."

It was the tone of voice that made Darlene realize she had lost. She always lost when her mother used that tone of voice. So, she let her mother pull back the covers. Her fears had come true, she had bloodied the sheets.

"I thought so," her mother said. "It's bad enough that Justine turned out to be a tramp, but now I have to worry about you as well. You're no longer a little girl and now you have to remember something very important. Don't you ever let a boy put his thing inside you or you'll be sorry."

There were tears in her mother's eyes as she said this, and for a moment, Darlene felt sorry for her. But then her mother was standing up, assuming her familiar military-style posture and telling her to come into the bathroom with her. She gave her something she called a belt and showed her how to attach a thick pad to the belt. She turned to leave the room but then hesitated and turned back. She gave Darlene one of her sternest looks, pointed a finger at her, and warned, "Mark my words, Darlene. You'll be sorry if you ever let a boy put his thing inside you." Then she was gone.

Darlene's stomach still hurt but something else inside her was hurting as well. She didn't know what this something else was, except that it had something to do with the look on her mother's face and that she never, ever wanted to feel it again. Then she switched her attention to the problem at hand. Was she supposed to use the same pad all day while at school? What if she had an accident? She would rather die than have anyone know she was having her period. She would have to take an extra pad, but where would she carry it? It was bulky and wouldn't fit into her purse. Besides, someone might see it there. Then she got an idea. She went into the kitchen, got a brown lunch bag, put the pad inside the bag, and then put the lunch bag into her book bag. Anyone who might happen to see it would think it was just a regular lunch bag.

Her stomach continued to bother her all day, and worrying about having an accident didn't help matters. She kept going into the bathroom, checking to see if she needed to change the pad. By eleven o'clock in the morning, she knew she was in trouble. She had only brought one extra pad and she couldn't put off changing it any longer. But if she changed it now, would she make it through until the end of school? Another crisis hit when her gym period rolled around at two o'clock. She panicked at the thought of undressing in front of the other girls. Someone would notice for sure. She went to her gym teacher and told her she wasn't feeling well. She was caught totally off guard when her teacher looked her straight in the eyes and asked her if she was having her period.

Darlene felt her pulse quicken. She wasn't accustomed to lying, but after the things her mother had said, she was afraid to tell the truth. If she lied, however, she might have to undress. She ended up mumbling a weak yes. To her surprise, her teacher simply asked her if she was having cramps. Again, Darlene managed a weak yes. What happened next was even more of a shock. Her teacher told her there were some pills that would make her feel better and more pads in the nurse's office if she needed them. Darlene didn't know what to think. This woman was acting as if having a period was the most natural thing in the world. It was all very confusing, but nonetheless she was glad to have access to another pad and delighted to find that the pill made her feel much better.

Several months later, Justine was back, reappearing as

suddenly as she had disappeared. Darlene thought the fighting might return and was relieved and confused when she discovered that there was absolutely no communication at all between her sister and her parents. The silence at the dinner table seemed uncomfortable for everyone, but nobody seemed willing to do anything about it. Darlene was afraid she would say something wrong, so she kept quiet as well.

Justine seemed like a changed person. She no longer smiled and didn't even bother to tease Darlene, which seemed very strange after so many years of enduring her taunts. Justine had not returned to school, so when she turned eighteen she left home and, within a year, left the state as well. Her parents acted as if Justine had never existed; they never once mentioned her name, at least as far as Darlene could tell. Contact between the two sisters was limited to an occasional birthday card. It would be several years before Darlene would learn exactly what had happened.

About five years after Justine left home, she returned for a visit at Christmastime. She arrived on the doorstep with a husband and a new baby. At first, Darlene was very nervous about how her parents might react, so she was relieved when they seemed pleased to see Justine and welcomed her home. It was during this visit that Justine told Darlene exactly what had happened when she was seventeen.

When Darlene heard that her sister had become pregnant, had been sent away to have the baby, and then had been forced to give the child up for adoption, she found she wasn't at all surprised. Deep down she had always known that the rift between Justine and her parents had something to do with sex and with babies. At the time, she had been too young and too ignorant to put it together in her mind, but over time she had come to suspect that Justine had been punished for letting some boy have his way. While Justine was telling her story, she was holding her new baby in her lap. It momentarily crossed Darlene's mind that another man must have had his way with Justine as well. She assumed, however, that, because they were married, it was now okay. Obviously, she thought, marriage made sex with a man acceptable.

As the events in Darlene's life unfolded, it became more apparent why she had developed an intense aversive reaction to penetration. A set of early unpleasant experiences had made her more vulnerable than others to developing a phobia.

Darlene had been primed by her mother to believe that girls who let boys have their way with them were nothing more than tramps. Then, indirectly, she experienced the angry, rejecting consequences of her sister letting a boy have his way. Immediately following her sister's banishment, she began her menstrual period and was chastised and therefore, in her mind, rejected by her mother (as her sister had been rejected). Both the blood from her menses and "letting a boy put his thing in you" were now firmly associated with shame and with the fear of being rejected.

Then Harold entered the picture. She was in love with Harold, but he seemed primarily interested in what Darlene had been warned against. Darlene wanted to keep Harold, but she had been taught that intercourse with a boy resulted in banishment and rejection. She refused to let Harold have his way with her and, in the ultimate irony, was rejected anyway.

Later, Harold reentered her life. Thinking that her earlier choice of abstinence had not saved her from rejection, this time she decided to make the opposite choice. But the closer she got to the reality of penetration, the stronger the associated feelings of shame and rejection became. At the actual moment of penetration, Darlene felt only panic and a desire for escape. Unable to flee, she experienced yet another fear: suffocation.

She survived the feeling of suffocation only to be confronted with the sight of blood, triggering once again her
fear of rejection. As she anticipated that Harold would reject her because she allowed him to "have his way" with
her, panic recurred. Of course, in the end her fears came
true: Penetration *did* equal shame plus rejection, just as her
mother had warned her. A classic phobiclike response to
penetration had been created. So strong were shame, rejection, and the feeling of suffocation associated with penetration that even the sanction of marriage and the passing of
years were unable to break the connection.

Believing that marriage would, in fact, make her fear of
penetration go away, Darlene had been able to convince
Jake that eventually they would have normal sex. After all,
marriage had made things right for Justine, so why
wouldn't it make things right for her? But when marriage
didn't take away her fears, another apprehension was
added to her life. Darlene woke each morning with the
thought that today would be the day Jake would get fed up
and leave. Each evening when he walked into the house,
she breathed a sigh of relief. During the years Jake had
been so strung out on coke, it had never once occurred to
Darlene that *she* might be the one to leave. After all, she
was damaged goods and marriage had not magically
changed that.

Again and again she had promised Jake that she would
do something about her problem. But as his drug use escalated, it took the focus off her problem and allowed her
to procrastinate. Years later, when he got clean, she finally
took a step toward confronting her fears and made the appointment with the physician/sex therapist. But she had
panicked when he tried to do the exam, and this had
stripped her of the little confidence she had mustered. The
incident had served to prove to Darlene that she wasn't
ready to confront her fear. Several years went by, and although Darlene made more promises to herself and to Jake,
she did nothing. Then the letter from the reunion commit-

tee came. When Darlene saw Harold's name at the bottom, something inside of her was triggered. She wanted to stop being afraid. She wanted to have a normal sex life. And she wanted to face Harold.

Once Darlene and I understood all that went into creating her problem, we were ready to strip it of its power, one step at a time. Her fear had to be chipped away in increments that she could handle. This would take time. I tried to convince Darlene that it would be important for her to keep the pressure off by avoiding an artificial time frame, but she was insistent. "I can do it," she said again and again. "I can be free of this problem in time to smile at Harold and genuinely mean it."

"Harold's only a symbol to you. It's not Harold you have to confront, but what he represents: shame and rejection."

"I understand that now and I'm ready to begin."

Vaginismus is treated by desensitization, in which vaginal dilators of varying sizes are used. Desensitization is a treatment technique built upon the idea that fears can be graded from less fearful to most fearful. The person is gradually exposed by degrees (from lesser to greater) to the feared situation. The dilators are stainless-steel rod-shaped objects of varying diameters. The idea would be for Darlene to conquer her fear of penetration a little at a time by starting with the smallest dilator, about the size of a pencil, and progressing until she was able to insert a dilator the size of an erect penis. Desensitization uses the success of the previous accomplishment as encouragement to conquer the next, more fearful, situation.

In Darlene's case, her problem was more than just a fear of pain at the idea of penetration. Penetration had also come to mean rejection and abandonment. In Darlene's unconscious mind, she was convinced that if she had intercourse with Jake, he would leave her. So, the treatment had to accomplish two goals: It had to break through her connection of penetration with both physical and emotional pain.

Guided imagery is often helpful in both of these treatment goals. With guided imagery, relaxation techniques are used to put the patient in a relaxed state. Then the therapist talks the patient through the situation while the patient imagines herself accomplishing the desired goal. With Darlene, guided imagery was used at each step along the dilation process. In each step she mentally saw herself being able to insert the dilator without pain and with Jake always by her side. Audiotapes of the imagery sessions were made while Darlene was in my office. She took the tapes and could then listen to them as many times as she needed prior to practicing the dilation progressions at home.

Since the incident with Harold, nothing, not even a tampon, had trespassed Darlene's vagina. And the longer the problem went untreated, the more ingrained it became. Given these two facts, I was sure there would be a great deal of involuntary resistance from Darlene. No matter how motivated she was, conquering these fears would not be easy. So I wasn't surprised to find her visibly shaken when she came back the next week.

"I listened to the tape four times before I tried the dilator. I felt sure I could do it because I could see it happening in my head. But when I got the dilator near the entrance to my vagina, my body went rigid and the fear jumped out of nowhere right at me."

"Don't be discouraged. Desensitization means working with your fears a little at a time until you feel they're manageable. It also means being forgiving of yourself if you fail. Otherwise you'll increase, not decrease, the fear."

This process went on for many more weeks. Each time she was in the office, Darlene felt convinced she would be able to insert the dilator, and each time she tried it at home her body would become rigid and she could only get the dilator as far as the entrance to the vagina before her muscles would involuntarily clamp down, making penetration impossible. Her feelings of frustration and failure mounted, and no matter how much I reminded Darlene that she was sabotaging herself with the time pressure, she refused to give up on her deadline, which was now only four months away.

Then it happened. Somewhere around the fifth or sixth week of trying, Darlene was able to get the dilator about an inch and a half inside her. The next day she tried it, she was able to insert it several more inches. When she returned to my office the following week, she had a big smile on her face. "When it first slipped in, I could feel my body tense up, but I kept hearing your voice talking to me, telling me to breathe deeply and let all the tension out. Then, suddenly, it was really inside of me. I started to get that feeling of suffocation but I concentrated on breathing deeply. Then the suffocating feeling started to go away, and I just lay there with the dilator inside of me, thinking that nothing terrible had happened. I practiced several more times and each time it became easier and easier. Now it seems strange that I was so afraid. I'm ready to move on—to try a larger dilator."

Darlene did move on but was disappointed to find that with each new size of the dilator, she had to "start over again." The fear returned each time she increased the size of the dilator, and her body would involuntarily resist each new attempt. It was taking weeks for her to make progress, and she was feeling discouraged. I kept reminding her of how far she had come and that she was making remarkable progress as she now had only one-size dilator left. But Darlene still had only one measurement of success in mind— staring Harold straight in the eyes—and now the reunion was only two months away.

The normal progression in the treatment of vaginismus is to work through the various-size dilators with the woman in complete control of insertion. Feeling out of control is often what initiates the panicky feelings. Almost always with intercourse the man is larger, stronger, and, therefore, more powerful than the woman. In addition, it is usually the man who does the insertion. All of these factors contribute to the woman's feeling out of control.

At this point in the treatment program, I suggested to Darlene that Jake be included in her progress. He was to be with her when she tried the largest of the dilators, but not to participate in the insertion. Even though she knew this was the normal progression of treatment, she became anxious at the idea of Jake being present. I told her that her anxiety was completely normal and reminded her of how anxious she had been at the beginning when she tackled the very first dilator. She smiled at the recollection and acknowledged that this experience was likely to move along in the same way. And it probably would have, except for her insistence on success within a limited time frame.

Darlene had a big calendar she was using to mark off the days until the reunion. She also used the calendar to indicate successes in her treatment program. Gold stars had been pasted on the days in which she had made progress with the dilators. However, when she flipped the calendar over to the month in which the reunion was to take place, she began to get overly anxious about accomplishing her goal in the time that was left. She started having trouble sleeping at night because of dreams about the reunion. She would wake up shaking with fear from dreams about Harold, who was either laughing at her or ignoring her. Concentrating on her work became difficult; in fact, getting through each day became difficult. She felt irritable and often took this out on Jake.

Then one day, less than three weeks before the reunion, when she was leaving the bank where she worked, she saw a man in the parking lot. He was a fair distance from her but she thought he looked familiar. She kept walking toward her car, trying to place him. Since he was walking in her direction, the gap between them was quickly closing. When he was within about twenty-five feet, she froze. She was sure it was Harold. Even though she hadn't seen him in more than fifteen years, she felt certain it was Harold because his face had never left her memory. A great sense of disappointment mixed with fear gripped her, and she immediately started to feel the familiar fear of suffocation as well. She knew she was beginning to hyperventilate, and she could feel her legs weaken. Any second, she thought, she would faint.

Even though she was light-headed, her mind kept focusing on one thought: This was not how it was supposed to be. She had planned for almost a year to be ready to face Harold, no longer afraid of what he represented. Instead, she was going to make a fool of herself once more again by fainting right in front of him. It just couldn't happen this way, she decided. It would be too unfair. She would have to face him with dignity, even though she hadn't accomplished her goal. Now he was only a few feet away and she took a deep breath and said, "Hello, Harold."

The man looked at her for a moment as if to give consideration to whether he knew her. Finally, he said, "You must be mistaking me for someone else. I was just going to ask for directions to the convention center. Can you tell me how to get there?"

Darlene stared at him for a moment, blinking her eyes several times and trying to get her bearings. Her mind must have been playing tricks on her, she realized, because now he was standing right in front of her, he didn't look anything like Harold. She was puzzled as to how she got so confused but couldn't focus on that at the moment because he was again asking her directions to the convention center. He must think I'm some sort of idiot, she thought. Then she pointed down the street and said, "It's about two blocks in that direction. You'll see it right after you pass the big hotel."

The man thanked her and began walking in the direction Darlene had pointed. She watched him leave, aware that she felt foolish but also greatly relieved. She shook her head at the ridiculousness of the situation she had just fabricated. Obviously, the stress was getting to her. It was probably true after all, she thought, that putting an artificial timetable on her goal was not a good idea. While driving home she questioned why it had seemed so important to her in the first place. When she didn't come up with a good answer, she convinced herself that she could go to the reunion even if she hadn't licked her problem.

That night she dreamed about the man in the parking lot. In her dream the man turned out to be Harold after all. Darlene was composed and charming as she greeted him, and he was obviously impressed by her, asking her to join him for a drink. They walked to the nearby hotel. From the moment Harold recognized her, he had been unable to take his eyes off her, repeatedly complimenting her on how good she looked. Lightheartedly, he chastised himself for having let her get away. Then he went on to talk (and talk) about himself. The entire time she was with him, Darlene had felt an internal confidence, bordering on superiority, which allowed her to notice that Harold was rather insipid. She wondered what she had ever seen in him in the first place. Someone touched her shoulder and she turned to find Jake standing by her side. She introduced Harold to Jake and then excused herself, saying she and Jake had commitments elsewhere. She stood, kissed Jake hard on the mouth, and walked away. She was more in love with Jake at that moment than she had ever been in her life.

The dream was fresh in her mind when she woke the next morning, yet the confidence she had felt driving home the day before and in her dream seemed to have been stolen during the night. She felt robbed. How could all that resolve have slipped away? she wondered. Why was she once again feeling the urgency of accomplishing her goal before the reunion? She felt a tremendous surge of frustration at the whole damn process. Next, she felt a determination beyond anything she had experienced before. Her fears about intercourse had ruined her life for too damn long. Forget about step-by-step desensitization, she thought. Tonight she and Jake would do it.

She left work early, justifying her actions with the thought that she wasn't much use to anyone anyway. All she could think about that day was what was to take place that night. The strong determination she had felt earlier was now mixed with a low-level anxiety that was unfortunately counteracting her mission. To keep her resolve, Darlene reminded herself again and again that she was tired of having given in to her fears for so long. "Tired" wasn't exactly the right word. "Fed up" was more accurate. Never before had she felt such a commitment to ending her long ordeal. She knew she had to act while she was charged with purpose. She just wished she wasn't feeling so scared.

She thought a little romance might bring back her confidence. Besides, setting the mood would give her something to do. She cooked a nice dinner, lit some candles, and dressed in something obviously alluring. Even after nine years of dealing with "her" problem, Jake had never failed to assure her that he thought her body was terrific. How truly lucky she was to have him. This thought helped more than anything to spur her on. So when Jake walked through the door, some of her earlier confidence did return, especially after he gave a long, low whistle indicating he liked what he saw.

He didn't ask any questions, preferring, instead, to enjoy Darlene's efforts at setting a nice mood for dinner. For this she felt thankful. But as the meal drew to a close, Darlene could feel her anxiety begin to rise. Instinctively, she wanted to put on her old, worn robe and go read a book. What a natural, easy thing that would be to do. For the first time in all these years, she clearly saw how skillful she had become at undermining potentially sexual moments. The urge to run away, to avoid confronting her inadequacy, was as strong as ever, but this time she didn't give in.

Instead, she reached over and took Jake's hand. With a deep breath, she said, "Let's make love."

Jake smiled warmly and looked into Darlene's eyes.

Gently squeezing her hand he said, "You've never said that to me before."

Darlene stood up from the table, pulling Jake up with her. But when she started for the bedroom, she felt Jake resisting her forward movement.

"Darlene, I don't have to tell you how much I want this for us. But I want it to be right for you. You've been obsessed with this reunion thing and you may be pushing yourself before you're ready."

"I've never felt stronger in my determination than right now. Could it be wrong for us to savor the moment?"

"I don't know," he answered.

"Neither do I. But I have to try."

As he had been since he kicked the drug habit, Jake was slow and gentle with Darlene. It had taken Darlene a long time to trust that Jake had actually changed. When he was strung out on drugs, he had been easily aroused, driven for release, and practically oblivious to her. More often than not, however, there had been failures, which usually resulted in violent outbursts of frustration. But things really were different now. Jake was loving and tender and genuinely enjoyed pleasing her. She knew she was a difficult case. Frequently, it took her a long time to relax; experience had taught her that when she wasn't relaxed, her nerve endings felt dead and Jake might as well have been making love to a corpse.

But there were rare times, like tonight, when his touch felt electric, shooting bursts of erotic sensations through her body. There was something incredibly powerful about these sensations, a feeling that always made Darlene uncomfortable. Sometimes she would simply turn off the "electricity" as if it were a light switch, and her body would shut down. But occasionally she actually stopped trying to control the powerful feelings, letting the "electricity" flow and fill the reservoir of her body with pleasure until the dam broke. Always, however, when she let it go this far, she would end up crying after it was over. She felt helpless to do anything else because she was overwhelmed by mixed emotion. Until she had started therapy, she simply didn't understand how something that felt so good could also have made her feel so horrible.

Tonight was different. Tonight she was letting the powerful feelings through and knew she would not feel regret. Tonight she was going to change her life forever. More ready than she had ever been, she rolled on top of Jake, feeling his hardness pressing against her pelvis. It would be so simple, she thought, just to slip him inside her. So when she mounted him and could feel his penis pulsating in her hand she was totally unprepared for the panic that clutched at her chest, causing her to gasp for air and momentarily to be taken back in time. It was only Jake's cry of agony that caused her to return to the room and the realization that she had his penis to tightly clenched in her fist that he was in terrible pain.

She immediately let go of him and climbed off, flinging her body down on the bed beside him. She wanted to scream. Everything had been perfect and still she had ruined it. She could feel her frustration mounting and wished she had something to throw. Just then she heard a strange sound coming from Jake. At first she wasn't sure what it was, but then she decided it was a definite giggle. Furious that he would even consider such a thing, she sat up in bed and gave him a harsh look. This only seemed to intensify his laughter which, to her surprise, felt suddenly contagious. Before she knew it, the two of them were involved in an uncontrollable fit of laughter.

In the session after this incident, Darlene walked into my office with the brightest of smiles. "You were right, you know. Putting all that pressure on myself did backfire." And she proceeded to tell me all that had happened from the day she thought she saw Harold in the parking lot to the night she inadvertently almost destroyed a necessary part of the solution to her problem. When she finished, she leaned back in her chair and smiled once again. "I've heard about the healing nature of laughter, but it took that night for me to understand just how powerful it can be. It gave me a whole new perspective on the problem. The reunion is now two weeks away, but I no longer feel obsessed. I know I'm going to lick this thing because Jake is truly by my side for good. I've been so afraid to trust that he, too, wouldn't abandon me, but after surviving that night I started believing he's not going to leave."

With these last words, I knew Darlene was going to get what she wanted. She had conquered her fears of abandonment and she was just about through the process of dilation. All she needed now was patience, and I could tell from her attitude that she now had that as well.

"You've been telling me all along," she continued, "that it's not Harold but me I have to prove something to, and that I could take whatever time I need to resolve my fears. Intellectually, I've known you were right. But what I couldn't do was let go of wanting revenge. I'm ready to do that now."

"Revenge is very seductive," I said, "because it's based on blaming someone else. Blaming allows us not to take responsibility for our shortcomings. Apparently, it's very instinctive behavior. Children do it all the time when they say, 'She started it' or 'He did it first.' Few of us outgrow our need to blame someone else.

"It's not that Harold didn't treat you badly, it's just that blaming him solves nothing."

"I just didn't want to let go of the fantasy of Harold regretting the way he treated me. But I don't need it anymore." Then she gave me one of her winning smiles and added, "However, that won't stop me from buying the sexiest dress I can find."

Nervous but determined, Darlene made a point of seeking Harold out at the reunion. In many ways, she later told me, their meeting was a reenactment of her dream. She proudly introduced Jake to Harold, and after some small talk, Harold leaned over and whispered in her ear that he was a fool to have let her get away. It was very satisfying for me to see the gleam in her eye as she told me her response: "I told him it may have been his loss, but it was certainly my gain."

After the reunion, Darlene's resolve to rid herself of her problem grew even stronger. She made an appointment with a gynecologist to have a pelvic exam, something she had avoided for twenty years. We talked on the phone the morning of the exam, and she admitted to feeling panicky but nevertheless determined. She called me after the exam, and I could hear the pride in her voice as she talked about managing her fear during the exam.

Resolution of her problem was just around the corner. Her step-by-step successes were giving her confidence, and Jake threw in an additional motivator: a second chance for a Hawaiian honeymoon, their first one having ended in disappointment and arguments.

About a month after the reunion, Darlene announced she was ready to substitute the "real thing" for the dilators. Again, her determination was obvious. Several unsuccessful attempts, however, resulted in some frustration.

"Just as he's about to penetrate, I feel flooded with fear and my legs tighten up and then Jake can't get in. He says my face is filled with fear, and he knows I'm not ready so he just withdraws. Why is this taking so long? I should be way past this now."

I reminded her that she had met roadblocks like these at each step along the way. "If you focus on your failures instead of your successes, you'll sabotage yourself. Think about how far you've come since you started."

Several more months went by with Jake and Darlene making little progress. Still, Darlene never once said she felt hopeless or wanted to quit trying. Then one afternoon she walked into my office and handed me an envelope. Inside were two tickets to Hawaii. I looked up at her and she was radiating one of those beautiful smiles of hers. ''It happened just like you said it would. We were doing the same thing we always do, and then I must have relaxed my legs and body because Jake was inside of me. It was scary, but I didn't feel panicky. I just concentrated on my breathing and relaxing my body. He withdrew after a minute or so, and then I started to feel a little sore. But it was a great feeling. I mean I didn't mind the discomfort at all because I was so excited at having done it. In fact, I was so thrilled, I insisted we do it again a couple of hours later—and we did. I felt a little sore all the next day, but I have to admit I 'wore' the soreness like a medal, a reminder of my victory.''

Darlene and Jake did have that honeymoon, although, at my suggestion, they delayed it for several months. Darlene had conquered her fear, but it would take time for her to relax and enjoy intercourse. However, with the kind of teamwork these two had developed, I knew it would be just that—a matter of time. And I was right.